QUADRILLE

QUADRILLE

A Romantic Comedy in Three Acts

by

NOËL COWARD

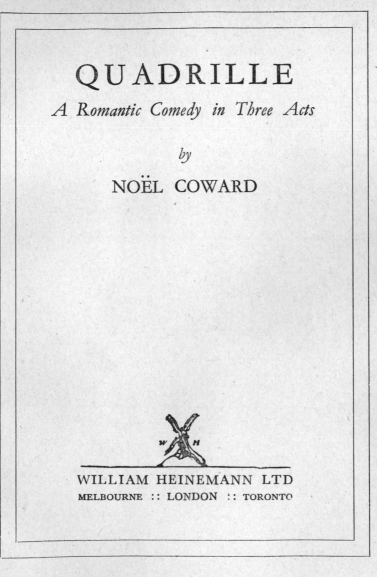

WILLIAM HEINEMANN LTD
MELBOURNE :: LONDON :: TORONTO

FIRST PUBLISHED 1952
—
PRINTED IN GREAT BRITAIN
AT THE WINDMILL PRESS
KINGSWOOD, SURREY

FOR

LYNN AND ALFRED

with more than thirty years of love
and admiration

Quadrille was first performed at the Opera House, Manchester, on July 15th, 1952.

CHARACTERS
(In the order of their appearance)

THE REV. EDGAR SPEVIN	JOHN GILL
SARAH (his wife)	MOYA NUGENT
GWENDOLYN (his daughter)	PAMELA GRANT
WAITER	MICHAEL ALLINSON
COURIER	TIMOTHY FORBES ADAM
THE MARQUESS OF HERONDEN (Hubert)	
	GRIFFITH JONES
MRS. AXEL DIENSEN (Charlotte)	MARIAN SPENCER
CATCHPOLE (a butler)	GORDON PHILLOTT
THE MARCHIONESS OF HERONDEN (Serena)	
	LYNN FONTANNE
LADY HARRIET RIPLEY	JOYCE CAREY
FOSTER (a maid)	SYBIL WISE
FOOTMAN	RHODERICK WALKER
AXEL DIENSEN	ALFRED LUNT
OCTAVIA, COUNTESS OF BONNINGTON	
	SYLVIA COLERIDGE
WAITER	CHARLES RENNISON
TRAVELLERS, ETC.	ALLEGRA NICOLE, DEREK PROUSE, BETTY HARE, GILLIAN RAINE, RICHARD SCOTT and DOROTHY BLYTHE

Directed by THE AUTHOR
With grateful acknowledgment to Miss Fontanne and Mr. Lunt.

Scenery and Costumes by CECIL BEATON.

SCENES

ACT I

ACT II

ACT III

Incidental music by NOËL COWARD.

Music under the direction of Leslie Bridgewater.

The Scene is the Buffet de la Gare, Boulogne.
The Time is May, 1873.

> *When the curtain rises it is very early morning and the gas-lamps are still burning. The sun has not yet risen but the grey daylight outside is brightening. There are a few tables discernible at which are seated travellers sipping coffee or chocolate. They may murmur to each other occasionally but this is rare because they are sleepy.*
>
> *A lady in black presides at the buffet bar at the back. She is aided by two waiters who scuttle about between the tables.*
>
> *At a table down right the* Reverend Edgar Spevin *is seated with his wife,* Sarah, *and their daughter,* Gwendolyn. *He is a harassed, bright little man; over-eager, amiable and, like certain types of dogs, trustingly convinced that everyone is delighted to see him.* Sarah *is as grey as the weather of her native Cumberland.* Gwendolyn, *aged fourteen, lacks charm to a remarkable degree. She is also a bad traveller.*

Gwen: It is coming on again, Mama.

Sarah: Not *again*, Gwendolyn!

Gwen (*tearfully*): I cannot help it, Mama. I think I am going to die.

Mr. S.: Come, come, child, that is no way to speak.

Seasickness is not a mortal disease, you know. A great number of people are seasick every day of the week.

GWEN: Oh, Papa!

SARAH: Really, Edgar. There is no necessity to harp on it.

MR. S.: I realise that it is unpleasant while it lasts but it doesn't last long once one is on dry land.

GWEN: It is lasting with me. It is coming on again now. I know it is.

MR. S.: You had better take her, my love.

SARAH: I don't know where it is.

MR. S.: I will enquire. (*He calls.*) Waiter—Garçon.

A WAITER *appears.*

WAITER: Monsieur?

MR. S.: Ma petite fille est souffrante. Ou est la lavabo?

WAITER: La deuxième porte à droite, Monsieur.

SARAH (*laboriously*): J'espére que c'est bien propre?

WAITER: Ca je ne sais pas, Madame. Ce n'est pas mon metier.

SARAH (*rising*): Come along, Gwendolyn.

GWEN: Hurry, Mama—please hurry.

They exit hurriedly.

WAITER: Encore du café?

MR. S.: Non, merci.—Well, perhaps half a cup—Oui, un peu encore.

The WAITER *fills his cup and darts off to another table. A group of people rise, having paid their bill—and go out on to the platform.*

As they go, a uniformed COURIER *comes in ushering effusively the* MARQUESS OF HERONDEN (HUBERT) *and* MRS. AXEL DIENSEN (CHARLOTTE). HUBERT *is a handsome man in the late forties. He looks the typical*

2

English "Milor" of the period. CHARLOTTE *is several years younger than* HUBERT. *She is exquisitely dressed, blonde and very carefully preserved.*

COURIER: This table is reserved, Milor.

HUBERT: Thank you.

COURIER: I will call you five minutes before the train leaves and conduct you to your compartment. (*He calls.*) Garçon.

    A WAITER *approaches.*

WAITER: Monsieur?

COURIER: You wish for coffee or chocolate, Milor— Milady?

CHARLOTTE: Oh dear.

HUBERT: I am travelling incognito. The name is Baxter-Ellis. A plain Monsieur will suffice. Coffee, please. Charlotte?

CHARLOTTE: Yes, coffee—anything.

HUBERT: Coffee, butter, croissants—vite.

WAITER: Bien, Monsieur. (*He bows and goes.*)

HUBERT (*to the* COURIER): Thank you for your help.

COURIER: A pleasure, Milor—an honour, Monsieur. (*He bows and goes.*)

CHARLOTTE (*after a pause*): Oh, Hubert!

HUBERT: My love, my pigeon—you are sure you wouldn't have preferred chocolate?

CHARLOTTE: It was not the thought of coffee that made me sigh.

HUBERT (*placing his hand over hers*): Look at me, Charlotte.

CHARLOTTE (*looking away*): No, Hubert.

HUBERT: I insist. Please.

CHARLOTTE (*reluctantly meeting his gaze*): There.

HUBERT: Remember our pact. Our spoken vow.

3

CHARLOTTE: Yes, Hubert.

HUBERT: No regrets. Whatever should happen, no regrets. That was a most solemn promise, my dear love.

CHARLOTTE: I know it was—but——

HUBERT: The past is over. We have the present, and the future.

CHARLOTTE: But the past is not over. Not quite over. There will be scenes and troubles, I know there will. Oh, Hubert, I am so afraid.

HUBERT: There will very likely be scenes and troubles, but not between us, we shall be far away. The sky will be blue above us and the Mediterranean will glitter in the sunlight. We will take breakfast on a terrace ablaze with bougainvillæa and scented with jasmine——

CHARLOTTE: Breakfast! Oh, Hubert!

The WAITER *appears with the coffee and croissants.*

HUBERT (*tenderly*): You are sure that you would not have preferred chocolate?

CHARLOTTE: Quite, quite sure.

HUBERT (*to the* WAITER): Merci.

WAITER: A votre service, Monsieur. (*He bows and goes.*)

HUBERT: What is done is done. There is no going back now.

CHARLOTTE: How long do you suppose it will be before—before——? (*She breaks off.*)

HUBERT: Before what, my heart?

CHARLOTTE: Before they discover where we have gone? Before they follow us?

HUBERT: I doubt if either of them will follow us, even if they do find out where we are.

CHARLOTTE: But Serena is a woman of strong character. You have frequently remarked upon it.

HUBERT: She has a will of iron.

CHARLOTTE: Oh, Hubert!

HUBERT: Her charm and her wit, which are considerable, mask an executive determination that would shame Napoleon Bonaparte.

CHARLOTTE: Please don't, Hubert. You are frightening me dreadfully.

HUBERT: She has absolutely petrified me for years. It has been most exhausting.

CHARLOTTE: She will undoubtedly follow us and petrify you again.

HUBERT: Never. I have escaped at last. And it is you who have delivered me. Your love is the file with which I have whittled down my prison bars, the knotted sheet by which I have lowered myself to freedom.

CHARLOTTE: Lowered yourself? How can you, Hubert!

HUBERT: A figure of speech, my love—my file—my lantern of hope in a dark and dangerous world.

CHARLOTTE: I sometimes wonder how much you really feel. Your phrases are so extravagant, so fanciful. Do they spring from your depths, these highly coloured words you use, or are they merely decoration, the icing on a cake, the flaking paint on old panelling?

HUBERT: Pray do not suspect me of dry-rot, my dearest.

CHARLOTTE: Am I your dearest? Has anyone ever been your dearest?

HUBERT: Do you anticipate betrayal already? Is your trust in me beginning to fade so soon?

CHARLOTTE: Your manner has been alar. ing ever since we left London Bridge.

HUBERT: In what way alarming?

CHARLOTTE: Too light, too irresponsible. You have been behaving like a bubble.

HUBERT: It is my lost youth that you have given back to me. I gazed at the smoky station and the hurrying people with new eyes. I listened to the escaping steam, the porters shouting, the whistles blowing, with new ears. I felt I wanted to shout and sing. It was only out of consideration for you that I refrained from bribing the engineer to allow me to drive the locomotive.

CHARLOTTE: Please do not speak of trains. I loathe them.

HUBERT: Forgive me. I had forgotten. How tactless of me.

CHARLOTTE: Railways are my husband's first love, last love and only love. I realised quite soon after our wedding that in marrying me he was committing bigamy. His heart and his allegiance belong to the Illinois Central. My married years have been flattened and deafened by the railways of the world. I too have, at last, escaped, only to find that my deliverer wishes to drive an engine. It is more than I can bear. (*She buries her face in her hands.*)

HUBERT: What can I say to retrieve my hideous blunder? What excuse can I give? The signals were against me and I crashed over the points.

CHARLOTTE: Hubert!

HUBERT: You must forgive this mood of mine, this reclaimed adolescence. Not only forgive but understand it, for after all it is your fault.

CHARLOTTE: How my fault?

6

HUBERT: Because of your stubborn, unconscious youthfulness.

CHARLOTTE: I am middle-aged, Hubert.

HUBERT: Never. One day, soon or late, you may suddenly be old, but never middle-aged.

CHARLOTTE (*with a smile*): How foolish you are.

HUBERT: Middle-age is an entracte, a tedious interval between the scenes when men and women of sensibility chatter in a vacuum, aware that what has so far happened is not enough, that there is more to come, that the curtain will rise again.

CHARLOTTE: Last acts are often tragic.

HUBERT: Comic too. A farce sometimes follows the sombre drama, or even a harlequinade, with clowns and columbines and pantaloons and strings of sausages.

CHARLOTTE: I had not envisaged the mellow years of our high romance as strings of sausages.

HUBERT: How touchy you are.

CHARLOTTE (*crossly*): Disillusion has begun all ready.

HUBERT (*apologetically*): My ill-considered words again, my wilful tongue, it was the sausages.

MR. SPEVIN *approaches their table*.

MR. S. (*diffidently*): Excuse me.

HUBERT: By all means. What have you done?

MR. S.: Intruded perhaps?

HUBERT: Perhaps. But surely not without reason?

MR. S.: You are the Marquis of Heronden?

HUBERT: Yes.

CHARLOTTE (*warningly*): Hubert.

HUBERT: The incognito is as yet less than skin deep. This gentleman could not be expected to salute it.

MR. S.: I recognised you, sir—my lord. I could not fail to. My name is Spevin.

7   B

HUBERT: Spevin—Spevin? Is that name then a symbol of clairvoyance? Has it a psychic affiliation of which I am unaware? How could you "not fail" to recognise me?

MR. S.: The village of Clanbury lies between two hills, my lord. It was my living for several years. Beyond the nearest hill is Heronden. My little daughter Gwendolyn's earliest memories are of the mushrooms in your park.

HUBERT: Not quite her earliest, surely?

MR. S.: To see you here, unexpectedly, among all this foreignness suddenly overcame my natural diffidence and inspired me to speak. Please forgive the impulse, it was too strong to be denied.

HUBERT: I forgive you freely. But having indulged your impulse, having abandoned yourself to this sudden urge, what is it that you wish to say?

MR. S.: I noticed on the steamer that your luggage was labelled "To Nice".

HUBERT: A man of uncanny observation. A very reverend detective. I tremble for your flock, Mr. Spevin.

MR. S.: That is the reason for my intrusion. My flock.

HUBERT: I cannot believe that a man so palpably sincere as yourself should deliberately wish to confuse me, but how, in the name of heaven, can a brief conversation with me in Boulogne concern your flock in Clanbury?

MR. S.: It isn't at Clanbury. It was, but it isn't any more.

HUBERT: Surely not a mass evacuation?

CHARLOTTE (*disapprovingly*): Really, Hubert——

8

HUBERT: It is disconcerting, my dear, to find oneself completely at sea ten minutes after landing.

MR. S.: I am the vicar of the English church at Nice, my lord. My predecessor there died in March.

HUBERT: A treacherous month, even on the Riviera.

MR. S.: My congregations are sparse, mostly residents, and nearly all of them invalids. I was wondering if I could prevail upon you to honour me with your patronage?

HUBERT: You would like me to come to your church? To set an example? To be an incentive to the laggards—that's it, isn't it?

MR. S.: Yes, my lord. It is quite a nice little church, architecturally primitive, of course, but pleasantly situated.

HUBERT: I will make no promises. My doctor has ordered me complete rest, and a public appearance, even among resident invalids, may be too much of a nervous strain. However, if I fail to come, you can count on me for a subscription at least.

MR. S.: It is most gracious of you, my lord, most kind.

HUBERT: The name is Baxter-Ellis.

MR. S. (*astonished*): Baxter-Ellis?

HUBERT: The address, Villa Zodiaque, St. Guillaume des Fleurs.

MR. S.: But I understood——

HUBERT: For various reasons, Mr. Spevin, I am travelling incognito. It is a whim of my doctors. A new name, he said, coupled with new surroundings and different sights and sounds, will work wonders.

MR. S.: I trust that your indisposition is not serious?

HUBERT: Fairly serious, I am afraid. (*He glances at*

CHARLOTTE.) A strange form of fever. It can cause considerable inconvenience although it is only rarely fatal.

CHARLOTTE: Hubert—the train—it is nearly time.

HUBERT (*firmly*): Au revoir, Mr. Spevin.

MR. S.: Thank you so much—you have been so kind —so kind.

MR. SPEVIN *bows rather tentatively to* CHARLOTTE *and most definitely to* HUBERT. *He then backs away and returns to his table.*

CHARLOTTE: How could you, Hubert? How could you so fluster the poor little man?

HUBERT: Certain people in the world are cunningly fashioned by the Almighty especially to bore their fellow creatures. Mr. Spevin is one of them.

CHARLOTTE: He was concerned for his church.

HUBERT: Only obliquely. His real motive was less worthy, a craving to hobnob, a desire to wave my title like a banner in the face of his ailing congregation.

CHARLOTTE: How cynical you are.

HUBERT: It is a matter of self preservation. Do you not realise what would happen if he were permitted to achieve his purpose? We should be lost, trapped in fearful gentility. Besides our secret would be discovered, our romance questioned and discussed and handed round the local tea-tables like petit fours.

CHARLOTTE: No English churchgoers will call on us, Hubert. Moral attitudes are more potent even than Marquisates. You seem to forget our sinful state.

HUBERT: Forget it! I was just glorying in it when that tedious ass came and interrupted us.

CHARLOTTE: The next year will be hard for me,

harder for me than for you. Society is lenient to men, especially eminent men, but I am a woman and an American.

HUBERT: To be a woman and an American! What greater gifts could God bestow?

CHARLOTTE: It is heartless of you to mock me. You are all I have to turn to now.

HUBERT: Is not my love enough to hold you safe? To secure you from little fears?

CHARLOTTE: It is not your love I doubt, but the world outside it.

HUBERT: We will have no traffic with the world outside it. We will be sufficient to each other.

CHARLOTTE: That is easy to say now, at the beginning. But later, when the excitement has simmered down, what then?

HUBERT: What then indeed!

CHARLOTTE: You are mocking again.

HUBERT: Is it a private hell of recrimination that you visualise? The two of us bitterly pecking out the feathers of the wings that once bore us away so bravely?

CHARLOTTE: There you go again, suffocating me with words.

HUBERT: Although we knelt before no altar, you have taken me for better or for worse.

CHARLOTTE: Let it be for better, Hubert, and please try to discuss our circumstances more simply. Whenever you embark on a sentence I feel as though you were off on a long journey and that I must wave you good-bye.

HUBERT: You are finding me a bore uncommonly soon.

CHARLOTTE: No, no—it isn't that——

HUBERT: Perhaps you would like me to recall Mr. Spevin. His phrases are flat enough.

CHARLOTTE: You are wilfully misunderstanding me.

HUBERT: I will speak in monosyllables from now onwards.

CHARLOTTE: You are unkind.

HUBERT: Dear love, this is our first quarrel. How charming! How exquisite!

CHARLOTTE: You are hopeless.

HUBERT: No, no—on the contrary—I am over the moon with hope and joy.

CHARLOTTE: Hubert!

HUBERT (*lyrically*): To be here with you, alone with you, actually to have the time to squabble. What bliss!

CHARLOTTE: Be quiet, Hubert, I beg of you. Mr. Spevin will hear you.

HUBERT: God bless him!

CHARLOTTE (*firmly*): Be quiet, Hubert. I will have no more of this. You will make us a laughing stock.

HUBERT: There speaks authentic Boston. Passionate courage and the dread of mockery.

CHARLOTTE: You know nothing of Boston. You have never been there.

HUBERT: I have read about it. Since our first meeting, since the first entrancing broad A I heard you utter fell on my ear, I have read nothing else. It is a city of magic to me. I could describe to you Beacon Hill on a snowy evening; the chill refinement of Back Bay. You will take me there one day. You shall be the first to show me the first families.

12

CHARLOTTE: Not until we are married, Hubert. Not until our divorces are over and done with and forgotten.

HUBERT: How wise you are, my sweetest heart. No Bostonian would receive us in our present state. I had foolishly forgotten their sturdy, New English rectitude. You shall return to your home a Marchioness.

CHARLOTTE (*covering her eyes with her hand*): Don't, Hubert. It may never happen.

HUBERT: It must. It shall.

CHARLOTTE: Serena will refuse to divorce you. I feel it in my bones. That is the fear that haunts me, the dreadful canker in my happiness.

HUBERT: Serena is a remarkable woman. She can be hard, forceful and determined, but there is no meanness in her. Also she has a tidy mind.

CHARLOTTE: A tidy mind?

HUBERT: She loves everything to be shipshape.

CHARLOTTE (*tartly*): Does she, indeed?

HUBERT: Her writing-desk is a model of neatness. Loose ends exasperate her. Life to Serena is insupportable unless it is spick and span, and nothing could be less spick and span than having a husband living abroad with someone else.

CHARLOTTE: Her passion for tidiness in no way prevented her from rising above your former infidelities with commendable fortitude.

HUBERT: You wound me, Charlotte. You really do.

CHARLOTTE: I am not quite a fool.

HUBERT: To think that all the time I was concentrating on Boston for your beloved sake, you were cross-questioning your friends about my former infidelities. It is heart-breaking.

CHARLOTTE: The fact remains, Serena acknowledged them.

HUBERT: She did no such thing. She placed them in a secret drawer in her mind marked "To be resolved later".

CHARLOTTE (*inexorably*): And they were.

HUBERT: Please, Charlotte, let us change the subject. This is most painful.

CHARLOTTE: Was divorce ever mentioned between you in those other earlier circumstances?

HUBERT: Certainly not. Nothing was ever mentioned between us. It was all tacitly understood.

CHARLOTTE: And will this, too, be tacitly understood? Something to be ignored, to be resolved later?

HUBERT: This is quite different. I have never loved before.

CHARLOTTE: Do not deceive me. I cannot bear it.

HUBERT: It is true. I have never before felt this enchantment, this lifting of the heart. This can never be resolved, later or at any time.

CHARLOTTE (*tearful again*): Oh, Hubert——

HUBERT: I have left Serena. I have left my life behind, gladly, ecstatically, to be with you until my last day. Serena will know that this is final, her instincts are sound and she is honest enough to admit defeat. But what if your husband should elect to play dog-in-the-manger? What if he should refuse to set you free?

CHARLOTTE: Axel will not refuse. He will not care enough. To him I am less than a locomotive.

HUBERT: A tender—a lonely, loving tender.

CHARLOTTE: It is no laughing matter.

HUBERT: It is now. All our past sadnesses are

laughing matters. Look into my eyes, my sweetest heart, and see the future mirrored in them, the sun and the stars and the lovely years that are waiting for us.

CHARLOTTE (*overwhelmed*): My darling.

They sit staring into each other's eyes. A bell clangs loudly outside. There is considerable activity in the buffet. MRS. SPEVIN *and* GWENDOLYN *come charging in.* MR. SPEVIN, *in a frenzy of agitation grabs them by the arms.*

MR. S.: Quickly—quickly—the train is going.

SARAH: The door stuck—we couldn't get out.

MR. S.: Never mind, you're out now.

SARAH: She was terribly sick again, poor mite. (*To* GWENDOLYN.) Pick up your bag, dear.

MR. S. (*breathlessly, as they collect their things*): I talked to them.

SARAH: Talked to who?

MR. S.: The Marquess and Marchioness, they were most agreeable.

SARAH: Marchioness indeed!

MR. S.: What do you mean, Sarah?

SARAH: That woman's not the Marchioness. I'd have recognised her on the boat if she had been

MR. S.: Her veil was lowered. I took it for granted.

SARAH: More fool you. Come along, Gwennie——

They rush out on to the platform.

The COURIER *returns.*

COURIER: The train is about to leave, my lord. If you will permit me I will escort you to your compartment.

HUBERT: Gladly. Charlotte?

CHARLOTTE: I am ready.

HUBERT: Really and truly ready?

CHARLOTTE: Yes, Hubert.

HUBERT: Come then.

HUBERT *and* CHARLOTTE *follow the* COURIER *out.*

There is a further clanging of a bell, the noise of whistles blowing and escaping steam.

CURTAIN.

The Heronden house in Belgrave Square.
The Scene is SERENA'S *private sitting-room.*
The time is five o'clock p.m. on the same day as the preceding
   scene.

   When the curtain rises CATCHPOLE, *an elderly butler,*
   is drawing the curtains back allowing the late afternoon
   sunlight to flood into the room. It is an exquisitely
   furnished room for SERENA *is a woman of great taste.*
   Somewhere on the other side of the Square a street organ
   is playing "The Last Rose of Summer".

   SERENA *enters followed by* LADY HARRIET RIPLEY.

   SERENA *is a striking woman. Her clothes are im-*
   peccable and there is something in her personality that
   commands immediate respect.

   HARRIET *is less impressive, of a lighter calibre. She*
   has been a cheerful widow for many years and her life is
   built on the affairs of her friends and acquaintances.

SERENA: I declare I am parched after all that horrid
dust. Bring tea at once, Catchpole.

CATCHPOLE: Very good, milady.

SERENA: I am not expecting any one, am I?

CATCHPOLE: I do not think so, milady.

HARRIET: What a relief! We can settle down to a nice
gossip.

SERENA: My dear Harriet, we gossiped incessantly
all the way to Richmond yesterday, all, or nearly all, the
time we were there and all the way back today. There
can be scarcely anyone left to discuss. (*To* CATCHPOLE.)

His Lordship left for Heronden last evening as arranged, Catchpole?

CATCHPOLE: Yes, milady. There is a note for you on the bureau. His Lordship wrote it immediately prior to his departure. He requested me to be sure that you received it safely.

SERENA (*glancing towards the bureau*): Doubtless something he forgot at the last minute. Thank you, Catchpole.

CATCHPOLE (*bowing*): Milady.

He goes out.

SERENA: It was sweet of you to come with me, Harriet. I fear that poor Mama is not exactly enlivening and that house is dreadfully oppressive.

HARRIET: She seemed happy enough I thought. It is the wretched Miss Godstone who commands my sympathy.

SERENA: Miss Godstone revels in subservience. She was born to slavery.

HARRIET: I should hate it so, being a companion, having to fetch and carry all day long, being utterly dependent.

SERENA: She was even more dependent in her own home. Imagine four brothers and five sisters all crushed into a small rectory in Suffolk. I expect Mama's draughty mausoleum at Richmond must seem a haven of rest by comparison.

HARRIET: Will Hubert be long away?

SERENA: Ten days at the utmost. He has to be back on the twenty-fifth for the Clavering's ball. I may join him towards the end of the week, a breath of sea air will revive me and Heronden is so lovely at this time of the year.

18

HARRIET: You do not look in need of revival. Your vitality always amazes me. I don't know how you do it.

SERENA: Do what, my dear?

HARRIET: All the things you do do. You are here, there and everywhere. Your charity committees alone would exhaust a more ordinary woman, then there are your other activities. How often have you dined peacefully at home during the last few years?

SERENA (*with a smile*): More often than you realise. At least once a fortnight. Foster brings me a tray in bed. I look forward to it.

HARRIET: Are you happy?

SERENA: What an extraordinary question. Why shouldn't I be?

HARRIET: I have no way of knowing. I merely asked if you were.

SERENA: You are quite irrepressible, Harriet.

HARRIET: Is it offensive to question the happiness of those one is fond of?

SERENA: No, not offensive, just a little startling perhaps.

HARRIET: Why startling?

SERENA: Because it gives a jolt to complacency, I suppose. A sudden query flung at random can pierce habitual armour most disconcertingly. It might even draw blood.

HARRIET (*persistently*): Did it? Did it draw blood?

SERENA (*laughing*): No, Harriet, no. Not even a tiny blue speck.

HARRIET: You admit however to being armoured.

SERENA: Of course I do. Our world can be treacherous.

HARRIET: What do you fear that causes you to take such stringent precautions?

SERENA: A million things, and there is nothing stringent about it. A façade is a necessary form of self-preservation. There is no mystery in it. I have little to hide.

HARRIET: What sort of things do you fear?

SERENA: Railway accidents, dogs being run over, going out on a winter's day without a handkerchief.

HARRIET: Now you are being frivolous.

SERENA (*continuing*): —dining at Windsor when the Queen is in one of her moods, standing wedged in the crowd at Covent Garden and watching my carriage drive away empty, having to sit next to Mr. Gladstone at luncheon——

HARRIET: Do stop.

SERENA: Most of all I fear being probed and prodded like some unfamiliar fish on a slab.

HARRIET: I accept the rebuke.

SERENA: It wasn't really a rebuke, and even if it were I know you far too well to hope that it would have the slightest effect. Ah, thank heaven here is tea at last.

CATCHPOLE *enters with a folding table and a cloth, followed by a young* FOOTMAN *bearing the tea-tray.*

HARRIET: The road just beyond Putney Heath is worse than I have ever known it.

SERENA: Quite abominable. I suppose the urban council is to blame. Someone should write a strong letter to *The Times*.

HARRIET: Perhaps you could persuade Hubert to do so. His name would carry great weight.

SERENA: Hubert never writes strong letters, he seldom writes letters at all if he can avoid it.

HARRIET: He has at least written you one and you haven't even opened it.

20

SERENA: I can guess only too easily what it contains. Probably instructions for his new riding boots to be sent on to him, or an engagement to play Whist at his club that he has forgotten to cancel. Restrain your curiosity until I have drunk a little tea, Harriet. I promise I will withhold nothing from you.

HARRIET (*irritably*): Really, Serena!

By this time the tea-table has been set—and CATCHPOLE *and the* FOOTMAN *have withdrawn from the room.*

SERENA (*presiding*): Now then—cream or milk?

HARRIET: Cream if you please.

SERENA (*pouring her out a cup of tea and handing it to her*): There are probably muffins in that covered dish.

HARRIET: Thank you.

SERENA: You look offended. Don't you care for muffins?

HARRIET: I am not offended. I am uneasy.

SERENA: Why?

HARRIET: There is something that I wish to say to you. At least I do not wish to exactly but I feel that it is my duty.

SERENA: That means that it is bound to be unpleasant. I shall have a muffin to fortify myself against the shock. (*She lifts the lid of the dish.*) Oh, how disappointing, it isn't muffins after all, only toast. (*She takes a piece.*)

HARRIET: I have been summoning up my courage to speak——

SERENA: Good heavens, is it as bad as that?

HARRIET: I do not know whether it is bad or not. I merely wish to put you on your guard. But you are so touchy sometimes, Serena. You are quite liable to bite my head off.

21

SERENA: Not with a mouth already full of toast.

HARRIET: It concerns Hubert.

SERENA: I suspected it did.

HARRIET: I saw him the day before yesterday.

SERENA: So did a number of people; he went to the Horse Show.

HARRIET: This was before the Horse Show, in the afternoon. (*She pauses.*)

SERENA: Well, Harriet, pray continue, I am on tenterhooks. What was he doing? It couldn't have been anything absolutely beyond the pale in the afternoon.

HARRIET: I saw him at the Zoo.

SERENA: He is devoted to the Zoo. So am I. Particularly when the seals are being fed. I dote on seals. They seem so carefree and they always appear to be applauding. If I were an actress I should like to perform to an audience exclusively composed of seals.

HARRIET: Hubert was not alone, Serena.

SERENA: It is difficult to be entirely alone at the Zoo. It is becoming more and more popular. Soon there will be so many people's heads in the way that we shall only be able to see the giraffes.

HARRIET: He was with a woman in a veil.

SERENA: A delicate skin no doubt. Some people freckle so easily.

HARRIET: You don't believe me?

SERENA: I most certainly believe you, as I sent them both on there after the brougham had dropped me off in Regent Street.

HARRIET (*deflated*): Both?

SERENA: The mysterious veiled lady was only poor Naomi.

22

HARRIET: Naomi?

SERENA: You must remember her, Naomi Charteris, Clara's eldest girl. She is Hubert's cousin once removed. As a matter of fact she was almost entirely removed last November when her horse rolled on her in the hunting field.

HARRIET: But——

SERENA (*mowing her down*): She came up from Kettering to have her teeth done and stayed three days with us. She has had to have a sort of contraption right across her mouth for months, poor child. That is why she wears a veil.

HARRIET: I see.

SERENA: She is a nice enough girl but self-conscious.

HARRIET: I am not surprised.

SERENA: She was never exactly a beauty at the best of times and of course being rolled on did little to improve her. However the doctor and the dentist say that she will be perfectly presentable eventually, so all's well that ends well.

HARRIET: It's no use, Serena.

SERENA: What is no use?

HARRIET: Trying to pull the wool over my eyes.

SERENA: I don't know what you mean.

HARRIET: Hubert's companion at the Zoo was not a gangling girl. She was a mature woman and extremely well dressed into the bargain.

SERENA: I wonder who it could have been then.

HARRIET: How much do you really mind?

SERENA (*sweetly*): Mind what, Harriet dear?

HARRIET: Hubert carrying on with other women?

SERENA: There is a perennial adolescence about you that is really most endearing. You always give me the feeling, when we are alone together, that we should be brushing our hair and sipping cocoa.

HARRIET: Well, really!

SERENA: After lights out, of course.

HARRIET: I respect your reticence, my dear, in fact I find it highly admirable but I must admit that it hurts me to realise how little you trust me. After all we are very old friends.

SERENA: If you respect and admire reticences so, why do you not accept it without being hurt? I have always had too much pride. It is my besetting sin. It is difficult for me to unburden my heart of its secrets, even to you, one of my closest friends. You will have to forgive me, Harriet, there are no two ways about it.

HARRIET (*wistfully*): In the old days, before we were both married, we used to discuss everything.

SERENA: You did, my dear.

HARRIET: My only desire is to help you, to be of some slight comfort if comfort is required.

SERENA: I know and I appreciate it most deeply. I will set your mind at rest over one thing at any rate. No comfort is required at the moment and if and when it is you will be the first that I shall turn to.

HARRIET (*a trifle waspishly*): At all events you cannot be emotionally upset after all these years.

SERENA: What a curious assumption. Would you like a little more tea?

HARRIET: No, thank you.

SERENA (*after a pause*): Oh dear, you are looking downright sullen. What *am* I to say to you?

HARRIET: I am sure you have a vast reserve of small talk. We could discuss the weather, the Wagner

Society, Miss Godstone's chilblains; you might even give me your views on the Albert Memorial.

SERENA: That would not be small talk, it would be high treason.

HARRIET (*rising*): If you think that I have been impertinent I can only assure you that it was quite unintentional and that I am sorry.

SERENA: Really, Harriet, this is too much of a good thing. Please sit down again immediately.

HARRIET: I would prefer to go now. I promised to call on Lavinia on my way home; she has moved into her new house. I am already late.

SERENA: I insist on you staying a few minutes longer. I cannot allow you to leave in anger.

HARRIET: I am not in the least angry.

SERENA: Nonsense, my dear. You are bristling like a hedgehog. If you happened to brush against Catchpole in the hall you would lacerate him. Sit down again, please. Hurt feelings between friends are intolerable. Please, Harriet.

HARRIET (*relenting*): Very well—just for a little longer. (*She sits down.*)

SERENA: What can I do to coax you back into benevolence?

HARRIET: Nothing.

SERENA: I have it—Hubert's letter! I will read it aloud to you.

HARRIET: I have no desire to hear it.

SERENA: But I want you to. (*She rises, goes over to the bureau, picks up the letter and returns to the tea-table, slitting the letter open as she does so.*) You can say ridingboots and I shall say Whist at the club and we will see who wins. (*She sits down and begins to read.*) "My dear.

I am afraid this letter will be a shock to you, but by the time you receive it I shall be——

She stops dead, reads on quickly for a moment, then, aware that HARRIET'S *eyes are on her, she bursts out laughing.*

HARRIET: What on earth is the matter?

SERENA (*now in perfect control*): He really is impossible.

HARRIET: What has happened?

SERENA (*playing for time*): You'll never believe it!

HARRIET: What is it? Why should the letter be a shock to you?

SERENA: Judge for yourself—listen—(*she pretends to read*)—"I am afraid this letter will be a shock to you but by the time you receive it I shall be safely at Heronden and out of reach of the first impact of your fury——

HARRIET: Good heavens!

SERENA (*still pretending to read*): Allow me, my dearest Serena, to make full and abject confession. (*She pauses.*)

HARRIET: Go on—go on. What *has* he done?

SERENA (*still pretending to read*): "I have sold the two small Romneys and the Gainsborough in the blue drawing-room to Sir Isaac Weissberger. He offered me so fantastic a price for them that I was unable to resist temptation. If you should desire either to divorce me or murder me I am entirely at your disposal. My love etc., etc." (*She folds the letter.*) There!

HARRIET: What an extraordinary thing to do.

SERENA: He must be demented.

HARRIET: Surely he is not in immediate need of money?

SERENA: Of course not.

HARRIET: Is the Gainsborough the one with the sheep in the foreground?

SERENA: The Gainsborough is the one with Hubert's great-grandmother in the foreground.

HARRIET: Who on earth is Sir Isaac Weissberger?

SERENA: I don't know. It is a very impressive name, don't you think?

HARRIET: What could have possessed him to do such a thing without even consulting you?

SERENA: There are many things that men do without consulting their wives. This is definitely one of them.

HARRIET: It sounds very fishy to me.

SERENA (*beginning to laugh, with a note of hysteria*): You are quite right. It certainly is fishy! Fishier than anything he has ever done before. Oh, dear——

HARRIET: Why are you laughing in that strange manner?

SERENA: I cannot help myself. (*She laughs with more abandon.*)

HARRIET (*alarmed*): Serena!

SERENA (*searching in her reticule for her handkerchief*): The situation has its humorous aspects.

HARRIET: Situation?

SERENA (*finding her handkerchief and dabbing her eyes*): Do not look so agitated, Harriet. I shall recover in a moment.

HARRIET: I think he has behaved irresponsibly and with utter lack of consideration.

SERENA: Yes, he has really, hasn't he?

HARRIET: And I cannot for the life of me see what there is to laugh at.

SERENA: Hubert's instability, his—unpredictableness, always make me laugh.

27

HARRIET: Why should he suddenly decide to sell three valuable family heirlooms without rhyme or reason? There must be something behind it.

SERENA: Not necessarily. Hubert's eccentricities are frequently quite motiveless. He has inherited a certain streak of waywardness from his mother.

HARRIET: Old Lady Heronden is not wayward, Serena, she is as mad as a hatter.

SERENA: You need not put it so crudely, Harriet. The family is prepared to admit that she suffers from rather curious delusions on occasion but beyond that they will not budge.

HARRIET: Facts are facts and there is no getting away from them. It is well known that she has imagined herself to be a bird for several years, and before that there were all those extraordinary letters she wrote to Lord Palmerston.

SERENA: The Albatross phase ended just after Christmas.

HARRIET: I'm sure I am very glad to hear of it.

SERENA: I believe that she is now something smaller and more manageable. I had a letter from Teresa only a week or so ago. It was guarded and far from explicit but I gathered from it that the situation had eased considerably.

HARRIET: I still do not see why the aberrations of Hubert's mother should be directly responsible for his abrupt disposal of two Romneys and a Gainsborough. Let me see the letter.

SERENA (*hurriedly*): No, Harriet. That would be a betrayal of confidence.

HARRIET: You have just read it aloud to me.

SERENA: That is entirely different. If Hubert ever

knew that you had actually read it with your own eyes he would be dreadfully humiliated. He is extremely sensitive about that sort of thing.

HARRIET: What was really in the letter, Serena?

SERENA (*shocked*): Harriet!

CATCHPOLE *enters with a card and a note on a salver.* What is it, Catchpole?

CATCHPOLE: Mr. Axel Diensen has called, milady.

SERENA: Mr. Axel Diensen? (*She looks at the card and opens and reads the note.*)

CATCHPOLE: I have shown him into the drawing-room, milady.

SERENA: Just a moment, Catchpole.

HARRIET (*to* CATCHPOLE): Is Mrs. Diensen with him?

CATCHPOLE: No, milady, he is alone.

HARRIET: How very odd.

SERENA (*thoughtfully putting the note back into the envelope*): You had better show Mr. Diensen up here, Catchpole. Solitude in the drawing-room can be depressing.

CATCHPOLE: Very good, milady.

He goes.

HARRIET: I didn't know that you knew the Diensens.

SERENA: I scarcely do. They were staying with Etta Tewkesbury when Hubert and I were there last autumn and I remember speaking a few words to them at the Cameron-Wilkinson wedding in February.

HARRIET: It was Etta who really launched them originally, wasn't it?

SERENA (*absently*): Yes. I believe it was.

HARRIET: She, Mrs. D., comes from Boston you know.

29

SERENA: Yes. She murmured it to me almost immediately on shaking hands. The significance of it escaped me at the time but I have since discovered that, in America, to come from Boston is essential.

HARRIET: He apparently is an entirely different proposition. Quite rugged I am told.

SERENA: Rugged?

HARRIET: He is a railway man and very rich indeed. I suppose I shall be snapped at again if I ask what was in the note?

SERENA: He wishes me to meet him secretly at the Zoo.

HARRIET: You are quite impossible today, Serena. This time I really shall leave you.

SERENA: Yes, you must. He says he wishes to see me privately on a matter of great urgency.

HARRIET: It is no use trying to tease me and tantalise me. I know perfectly well that it is a formal little note, probably from his wife, inviting you to a ball or to their box at the opera.

CATCHPOLE *enters.*

CATCHPOLE (*announcing*): Mr. Axel Diensen.

AXEL DIENSEN *enters. He is a tall, well-built man in the late forties.*

SERENA (*putting out her hand*): How do you do, Mr. Diensen.

AXEL (*taking it*): I am well, ma'am—thank you.

SERENA: This is Lady Harriet Ripley.

AXEL (*shaking hands with* HARRIET): I am honoured.

HARRIET: As a matter of fact we have met once before, for a brief moment, at that curious charity fête at Twickenham. Do you remember?

AXEL: Yes. I remember.

SERENA: Can I offer you some tea?

AXEL: No, thank you. My time is limited.

SERENA: In that case you had better leave the tea-things, Catchpole. Albert can come and clear them away when I ring.

CATCHPOLE: Very good, milady.

HARRIET: I really must go now, Serena, Lavinia will be furious. Good-bye, Mr. Diensen, I hope that we shall soon meet again.

AXEL: The pleasure would be mine, ma'am.

SERENA (*kissing her*): Good-bye, my dear. I will send you hourly bulletins.

HARRIET: How horrid you are.

    CATCHPOLE *ushers* HARRIET *out and follows her, closing the door behind him*.

SERENA: Pray sit down, Mr. Diensen.

AXEL: If you do not object, ma'am, I would prefer to stand, or even walk about.

SERENA: Perhaps you would prefer to return to the drawing-room? It is much larger.

AXEL (*moving to the window*): I am a man of action rather than words. The bulk of my life has been spent in very different circumstances to those in which I now find myself. I am well accustomed to handling men and making decisions and dealing with sudden crises when they occur—but not this sort of crisis.

SERENA: Crisis?

AXEL: Yes, ma'am. A most definite crisis.

SERENA: You alarm me, Mr. Diensen.

AXEL: You read my note?

SERENA: Yes.

AXEL: I said in it that I wished to see you on a matter of great urgency.

SERENA: Yes. I must admit that that puzzled me.

AXEL: You have no idea of what the matter might be?

SERENA: None.

AXEL (*violently*): Hell and damnation!

SERENA: Really, Mr. Diensen.

AXEL: Forgive me, ma'am. The railroads of the west provide inadequate training for the drawing-rooms of Belgravia.

SERENA: Be calm I beg of you. Your outburst startled rather than offended me. I am perfectly prepared to regard hell and damnation in the Biblical sense if it will make you any more comfortable.

AXEL: We are comparative strangers to each other.

SERENA: I fully realise that, but even comparative strangers might be able to discover some stretch of mutual ground, or should I say "track"? on which to meet, might they not?

AXEL: In this instance they most unfortunately have.

SERENA Unfortunately?

AXEL (*swinging away from her and striding about*): This is terrible—terrible——

SERENA: I can only hope, Mr. Diensen, for the sake of the American industrial progress, that you deal with your railroad crises with more dispatch than you are dealing with this one.

AXEL: I would rather face a faulty viaduct, a landslide, a collapsed tunnel, a forest fire and an engineers' strike, than tell you what I am obliged to tell you.

SERENA (*beginning to put two and two together*): Come to the point, Mr. Diensen.

AXEL: Has nothing happened to you today? Nothing unexpected?

SERENA: Happened to me?

AXEL: You have received no bad news? No news of any kind?

SERENA: I have been visiting my mother in Richmond. She has a slight cold.

AXEL: Since your return you have heard nothing? Received no disturbing message—no letter?

SERENA: Please say clearly and frankly what you have to say. Forget that I am a comparative stranger. Treat me as a board of directors, if you must, but for heaven's sake, speak.

AXEL: Hell and damnation! Hell and damnation!

SERENA: You said that before and it led us nowhere.

AXEL: Lady Heronden. (*He pauses.*) Your husband has left you.

SERENA (*looking at him steadily for a moment and then turning away*): Yes, yes, I know he has.

AXEL: You *know*?

SERENA: I understand your embarrassment, Mr. Diensen. I see clearly now what has happened.

AXEL: How long have you known?

SERENA: Only a little while, a few minutes before you arrived. I think I will sit down if you don't mind, we cannot both of us stroll about the room indefinitely. (*She sits down.*)

AXEL: I am deeply concerned, ma'am, deeply sympathetic, please believe that.

SERENA: Thank you, Mr. Diensen, you have my sympathy also. Hubert, my husband, left me a note which I received on my return from Richmond. It was brief, and mentioned no names. Your wife I presume was more explicit.

AXEL: Oh no. Her note said little beyond the fact

33

that she had left me, that by the time I received it she would be far away, and that she hoped that I would make no attempt to follow her. She mentioned no names either.

SERENA: Then how did you know, why were you so sure that my husband was the man she had eloped with?

AXEL: I guessed.

SERENA: Guessed?

AXEL: They have been seeing each other a good deal during the last few months.

SERENA: Have they? I didn't know.

AXEL: I discovered it only by chance, a few weeks ago; a friend of mine from Minnesota happened to meet them accidentally.

SERENA: At the Zoo?

AXEL: So you did know.

SERENA: No, that too was a guess. My husband has utilised the Zoo for a long while.

AXEL: I see.

SERENA: It is more convenient than the Tower of London, and less fashionable than Madame Tussauds.

AXEL: I think, after all, I will have a cup of tea.

SERENA: I will ring. (*She half rises.*)

AXEL: No, please don't ring, what is there will do.

SERENA: It is by now stone cold and quite black.

AXEL: Milk alone would be preferable to an interruption.

SERENA: I quite agree. (*She empties the remains of tea from* HARRIET'S *cup, washes it out with hot water over the slop basin, pours some milk into it and hands it to him.*)

AXEL: Thank you. (*He sits down.*)

SERENA (*pouring some out for herself*): I think I shall have some too.

34

AXEL: Once during a flood on the Aitcheson and Topeka, the train was stranded and I had to live on milk for two days.

SERENA: How fortunate to be able to procure milk in the middle of a flood.

AXEL: It was a cattle train.

SERENA: I see.

AXEL (*after a pause*): At the risk of being considered impertinent, may I say that I think you are behaving magnificently?

SERENA: I am not behaving at all.

AXEL: It must be a terrible blow.

SERENA: For you also.

AXEL: I have had longer to think about it. I received my note this morning. I, at least, have had the hours of the day in which to conquer my emotions and accustom my mind to the situation.

SERENA (*drily*): Time is a great healer.

AXEL: But for you the very suddenness of the blow must be shocking.

SERENA: Violent shocks are sometimes accompanied by a merciful numbness. I am told that in the heat of battle, for instance, soldiers frequently lose limbs without being in the least aware of it until afterwards.

AXEL: It is afterwards however that the pain begins.

SERENA: Have you been married for long, Mr. Diensen?

AXEL: Nearly nine years. My wife came from Boston, you know.

SERENA: I had heard of that enviable circumstance.

AXEL: She was an Elliot.

SERENA: How gratifying!

AXEL: Her family have always maintained that in marrying me she married beneath her.

SERENA: How undiscerning.

AXEL: Thank you, ma'am.

SERENA: Perhaps it will be a relief to them that she has eloped with a Marquess?

AXEL: In the circumstances I fear not. They are very strait-laced.

SERENA: Have you arrived at any decision, Mr. Diensen? Have you decided on any specific course of action?

AXEL: Certainly I have. That is the purpose of my visit. There is still time to avert complete catastrophe if we act immediately.

SERENA: Act immediately? What can we do?

AXEL: Go after them and bring them back.

SERENA: We don't know where they have gone!

AXEL: I do. They are at the Villa Zodiaque, St. Guillaume des Fleurs, Alpes Maritimes, France.

SERENA: How on earth do you know? How did you find out?

AXEL: Charlotte, my wife—she was baptized Charlotte by the way.

SERENA: An attractive name, provided it is not allowed to degenerate into Charley.

AXEL: It never has so far.

SERENA: Pray continue.

AXEL: I happened to give her a ruby and diamond necklace some years ago on the occasion of our second wedding anniversary.

SERENA: Very thoughtful.

AXEL: At the moment it is being re-set at a shop in Bond Street. She left secret instructions to her maid to forward it on to her by special courier.

SERENA: I expect she felt that she would be lonely without it.

AXEL: It was to be delivered to a Mrs. Baxter-Ellis at the address I have just told you.

SERENA (*thoughtfully*): Baxter-Ellis—Baxter-Ellis—— Ah, now I remember. Some years ago my husband was strongly attracted to a Mrs. Baxter-Ellis. You are quite sure of the name?

AXEL: Quite sure. I cross-examined the maid for two hours this morning. She finally broke down and confessed.

SERENA: I know the Villa Zodiaque. Hubert and I took it for the winter in 1865.

AXEL: You will accompany me there at once?

SERENA: Certainly not.

AXEL: But, Lady Heronden——

SERENA: It would be too humiliating, too—too vulgar. I couldn't consider it.

AXEL: Vulgarity be damned.

SERENA: It usually is, Mr. Diensen.

AXEL: Please, Lady Heronden, please be reasonable.

SERENA: Reasonable!

AXEL: Apart from you and me nobody knows as yet what has happened. The situation can still be saved.

SERENA (*suddenly rising and walking about the room*): This is intolerable—degrading——

AXEL: Do you love your husband, ma'am?

SERENA (*icily*): Really, Mr. Diensen. I think you go too far.

AXEL: Never mind about that—do you?

SERENA: Unlike your wife's maid, I shall not break down under cross-examination.

AXEL: But see here, Lady Heronden——

37

SERENA: As you said yourself. We are comparative strangers. I am not in the habit of discussing my private emotions with comparative strangers.

AXEL (*grimly*): Well, you'd better break your rule, ma'am.

SERENA: I am sure the railways of America owe a great deal to your blunt speech and your forceful character, Mr. Diensen, but kindly remember that I am not an American railway.

AXEL: You gave me permission just now to talk to you like a board of directors.

SERENA: It had not occurred to me that even *American* executives would be prepared to answer intimate personal questions in full committee.

AXEL: Committees are privileged, ma'am.

SERENA: Even so, privileges should not be abused.

AXEL: We are our own committee, a committee of two, and we are privileged to be in the hell of a difficult situation. Without plain speaking we shall get no place.

SERENA: As far as I can see there is no place to get.

AXEL: That is where you are wrong. The place for us to get is the south of France and quick at that.

SERENA: I have already told you that I have no intention of going to the south of France with you——

AXEL (*beginning to lose patience*): But listen a minute——

SERENA: There is nothing to prevent you going by yourself if you wish to.

AXEL: Don't you realise that we are in the same boat whether you like it or not?

SERENA: I do. And I *dis*like it intensely.

AXEL: Our only chance of averting scandal is to look facts in the face and pool our resources.

SERENA: I feel, Mr. Diensen, that our resources are too divergent to pool successfully.

AXEL: God give me patience!

SERENA: I find blasphemy offensive.

AXEL: That wasn't blasphemy, it was a heartfelt prayer.

SERENA: I really cannot feel that much can be achieved by continuing this conversation.

AXEL: But, Lady Heronden——

SERENA: That is all I have to say, Mr. Diensen.

AXEL: But why this? What have I done to offend you, to banish all reason from your mind?

SERENA: I am not accustomed to being spoken to in that tone.

AXEL (*striding about the room*): Hell and damnation! Hell and damnation!

SERENA: Your vocabulary seems to be as limited as your manners.

AXEL (*violently*): Wrong again, ma'am! Wrong all along the line! My vocabulary is boundless. I can curse the stars out of the sky with rich words that you do not even know exist. I can swear red, blue and purple for twenty minutes without repeating myself once! And it is only my manners that are restraining me from doing so now. They may be rough, these manners of mine which you dismiss with such aristocratic scorn; they may not be polished and shining and false like those of your careful little English world, but they were good enough for my mother and father, and they should be good enough for you too, because they come from the heart and are dictated neither by fashion nor snobbery. They at least prompted me to come to you immediately today, to try, quietly and reasonably to discover whether or not we might, in mutual understanding, decide together on a course of action. Then, for some frivolous reason best known to yourself, you suddenly get on to your high horse and start riding me down. I will not be ridden down, Lady Heronden, please make no mistake about that. I am not impressed either by your title, your position, or your traditions. I *was* impressed, up until a few moments ago, by your honesty and your intelligence. For the love of heaven, woman, what has got into you? I didn't ask if you loved your husband out of idle curiosity. It doesn't matter a nickel to me if you love him or not. All I wanted to find out was the degree of your affection for him, whether or not it was still strong enough to save him and his name and his reputation, from public opprobrium.

SERENA (*after a pause*): The meeting is now adjourned.

AXEL: Very well. I only ask your pardon for one thing, my vulgar impertinence in daring to call upon you. (*He bows and goes to the door.*)

SERENA: Mr. Diensen——

AXEL (*with his hand on the door handle*): Yes?

SERENA: Please do not go. The ill manners were on my side, not on yours. I am truly sorry.

AXEL (*still at the door*): It is my habit to speak my mind, ma'am, regardless of the company in which I find myself. This I know to be an error and I have tried to conquer it. My words do well enough when there is no urgency to roughen them, but when there is—— Oh Lord!—out they come like a river in full spate, and what little grace I have learned is swept away.

SERENA: Come away from the door, Mr. Diensen. If you flared up again you might vanish through it before

I had time to restrain you. You were right in what you said just now. We must pool our resources.

AXEL (*coming away from the door*): Bully for you, ma'am.

SERENA: You asked me if I loved my husband.

AXEL: Forget the question. It is of no consequence.

SERENA (*turning away from him*): The answer is "Yes" —very definitely "Yes". But I love him now without illusion. The years have banked down the fires leaving a pleasant, protective glow. He is a man of charm and wit and sensibility: he has a kind heart and is incurably romantic. His search for romance only began with me, whereas mine ended with him. He is also feckless and irresponsible to an alarming degree and, of course, excellent company. My life without him would be perhaps more tranquil but immeasurably dull.

AXEL: Thank you for your confidence, ma'am.

SERENA: And you? Can you tell me the state of your heart before we start on our journey? It would be a fair exchange. Are you in love with your wife?

AXEL: No, no longer in love with her. Time has banked down my fires also. But I am fond of her, too fond to allow her to break up her life if I can possibly prevent it. Society means much to her—a great deal too much as a matter of fact. The opinion of the world is as necessary to her as the sun is to a rose garden. If the sun withdraws and the wind blows cold, she will wilt considerably.

SERENA: We must both do our utmost to prevent her from wilting, Mr. Diensen. When do you propose to leave?

AXEL: Tonight.

SERENA: Tonight! Oh dear.

41

AXEL: I made all the necessary reservations early this afternoon in the hope that you would agree.

SERENA: You have told no one?

AXEL: No one. I have sent my wife's maid back to her home in Derbyshire. I myself have told the household that I am joining my wife on the continent for a few days.

SERENA: Hubert is supposed to be at Heronden, our house in Kent. Nobody will know that he isn't, for a few days at least. I shall explain to my maid and my butler that I am joining him there tonight.

AXEL: Surely your maid will expect to accompany you?

SERENA: Normally she would of course, but fortunately her sister is about to be married in Essex. I have been dreading having to make the gesture of letting her go. Now I welcome it. What time does the boat train leave?

AXEL: Eight o'clock p.m. from London Bridge station.

SERENA: Will you be so kind as to meet me at the barrier at seven-forty-five?

AXEL: I surely will, ma'am.

SERENA: Then that is settled.

AXEL: A deal, ma'am. (*He puts out his hand.*)

SERENA (*taking it solemnly*): A deal. Thank you, Mr. Diensen, for your consideration and also for your efficiency.

AXEL: Thank you, ma'am, for your understanding and your courage.

SERENA: The latter may fail me yet.

AXEL: I doubt that.

SERENA: Shall we succeed, do you think? Will this

curious campaign upon which we are embarking so impulsively be crowned with victory? Or shall we return with heavy hearts, shamed and humiliated and unable to meet each other's eyes?

AXEL: We shall at least have tried. To picture defeat at the outset will undermine our determination. We must banish the very idea from our minds. Death or glory, ma'am.

SERENA: A glowing phrase, Mr. Diensen, but in this particular instance, excessive.

AXEL: Until seven-forty-five, ma'am.

SERENA: Until seven-forty-five.

AXEL *bows and goes out swiftly.*

SERENA, *left alone, picks up* HUBERT'S *letter which she has left on the tea-table.*

She walks over to the window and looks absently out into the Square for a moment. Then she goes over to the bureau, tears the letter methodically into pieces and drops them into the waste-paper basket.

SERENA (*as she does so*): Hell and damnation! Hell and damnation!

CURTAIN.

ACT II: Scene 1

The Villa Zodiaque.

The main living-room of the Villa opens on to a terrace. The terrace commands a view of rolling hills crowned by small, sun-washed villages set among olives and cypresses. In the far distance is the blue line of the sea.

The room itself is spacious and pleasantly furnished in a mixture of styles, the predominant of which are sturdy Provençal and Italian rococo. There is naturally a sprinkling of Victoriana but the total effect, although confused, is charming enough.

Two nights and two days have elapsed since the preceding scene.

The time is mid-morning. Sunlight is flooding into the room and

> HUBERT *and* CHARLOTTE *are lingering over a late breakfast.* HUBERT *is attired in a splendid brocaded breakfast robe,* CHARLOTTE *is in a négligé.* HUBERT *is scanning the pages of* Le Petit Nicois.

HUBERT: It is not that I dislike "The Magic Flute", Charlotte, it is merely that it goes on for such a long time.

CHARLOTTE: I heard Jenny Lind sing it, she was exquisite.

HUBERT: To me she resembled an agreeably vocal currant bun.

CHARLOTTE: Hubert!

HUBERT: At all events she is not singing it this

44

evening in the Municipal Opera House. It is an un-
distinguished cast and not even a gala performance.

CHARLOTTE: It would be foolish anyhow for us to be
seen together at a gala performance.

HUBERT: Alas yes, but we cannot be furtive indefinitely. I had hoped that my love was strong enough
to still your social conscience.

CHARLOTTE: Social fiddlesticks, Hubert. My in-
sistence on discretion is for both our sakes; we are bound
to encounter unpleasantness sooner or later and it would
be silly to meet it half-way.

HUBERT: It shall be as you say, my precious dear.
We will stay in our fortress on our enchanted hill and
dine on the terrace in the moonlight. The nightingales
shall provide our opera; at least they will not sing
Mozart.

CHARLOTTE: I cannot bear you not to like Mozart.

HUBERT: For your sake my darling I will adore him, I
swear I will: your loving hand shall guide me to his
perfections. There will come a time when his every
mathematical semi-quaver will be clear pleasure to me,
but you must be patient; at the moment my heart is deaf
to all music save the sound of your voice. I have very
little ear anyhow.

CHARLOTTE: You are talking nonsense again.

HUBERT: When I was young it took me seven months
to learn "On the Banks of Allan Water".

CHARLOTTE (*rising impulsively and going over to the
windows*): It is no use.

HUBERT: What is no use?

CHARLOTTE (*turning*): Pretending.

HUBERT: Pretending what?

CHARLOTTE: That we are happy and carefree,

enclosed in a lovely private dream with no outside world to menace us and nothing to worry about.

HUBERT: Is your part of the dream wearing thin already?

CHARLOTTE (*in distress*): Yes—— Oh, yes it is.

HUBERT: A meagre little dream, barely more than forty winks.

CHARLOTTE: You will not admit it then?

HUBERT: Admit what?

CHARLOTTE: That there is a strain in the air.

HUBERT: Do be quiet, my dearest, you are frightening away the morning! It was clear and beautiful an hour ago, now there are clouds coming up over the sea, look, you can see them.

CHARLOTTE: We must go away.

HUBERT: We are away.

CHARLOTTE: Away from here I mean.

HUBERT: You are very fidgety, Charlotte, we have only just arrived.

CHARLOTTE: There are too many people near us here.

HUBERT: No one that we know, excepting poor old Octavia Bonnington.

CHARLOTTE: *I* do not know poor old Octavia Bonnington.

HUBERT: Then you shall, my tender heart. But I warn you she may alarm you.

CHARLOTTE (*protesting*): Hubert——

HUBERT: She lives in a dank villa just near-by and writes fiercely improper books under a pseudonym. None of her relations will have anything to do with her.

CHARLOTTE: Then why should we?

HUBERT: Because she is old and lonely and incurably sentimental. It would give her so much pleasure to

46

welcome two runaways, two ecstatic social outcasts.
We will call on her immediately, today.

CHARLOTTE: We will do no such thing.

HUBERT: Come, Charlotte, you must not be selfish.
We have happiness to spare, we are bathed in illicit
bliss! The least we can do is to share it.

CHARLOTTE: Share it! You must be mad.

HUBERT: Think what it would mean to her, an
elderly eccentric living alone with an ageing pug and a
curiously thick-set Major-Domo.

CHARLOTTE *twists her hands with irritation.*

CHARLOTTE: Hubert—— Oh, Hubert!

HUBERT (*enlarging on his theme*): Imagine her excitement! She would hear the sound of our carriage wheels
in the drive and, peering through quite dreadful
curtains, she would see us descend from it. She would
sense in an instant, from the way I touched your hand as
I helped you to alight, from the tenderness of your
smile as you closed your parasol, that we were in
love——

CHARLOTTE: Please stop, Hubert, I can bear no more.

HUBERT: In a moment she would be in the hall,
holding out her arms to us, warming her chilled old
heart in the flow of our passion: the pug would bark
wildly, the parrots would shriek—I forgot to tell you
that she has two vast macaws—rapture would flood
through the house. And all because two lovers, two
abandoned, wayward lovers, had suddenly appeared out
of the bright sunlight.

CHARLOTTE (*nearing the end of her tether*): Once and for
all, Hubert, will you stop talking! Your fantasies
are driving me mad, your endless words beat upon
my nerves until I want to scream. I will *not* consent

47

to call upon this Octavia whatever-her-name-is——

HUBERT: Bonnington.

CHARLOTTE (*moving about the room*): Oh—oh—oh!

HUBERT: Why do you say "Oh—oh—oh!" my treasure?

CHARLOTTE: Because I am lost. Because I am unhappy.

HUBERT: To the devil with Octavia Bonnington. Let her remain for ever in her sad tower gazing at an empty road.

CHARLOTTE: Oh, Hubert——

She bursts into tears.

HUBERT: Why do you weep so frequently, my angel? It is infinitely distressing to me.

CHARLOTTE: I have already told you. I am unhappy.

HUBERT: How can you be unhappy in Paradise?

CHARLOTTE: Perhaps because I am beginning to realise that it is a fool's Paradise.

HUBERT: Charlotte!

CHARLOTTE (*with spirit*): It is true. I am bewildered and insecure. I am deafened and blinded all the time by your exuberant romanticism. Our situation is difficult and, for me, haunted by the dread of humiliations. Your continued refusal to share my fears, your resolute determination to float through the air indefinitely, terrifies me. I am beginning to suspect that you are not in love with me at all, you are merely in love with the idea of being in love with somebody, anybody——

HUBERT: If I kissed you, would you forget my infamies?

CHARLOTTE: No.

HUBERT approaches her.

HUBERT: And forgive my verbosity?

48

CHARLOTTE: I do not wish you to kiss me.

HUBERT: Why not?

CHARLOTTE: Because it is not the moment. Mid-morning is no time for foolishness.

HUBERT: If it is the light that is worrying you we could draw the curtains.

CHARLOTTE: Really, Hubert!

HUBERT (*tenderly*): Please let me press my lips on yours, my darling.

CHARLOTTE: It would solve nothing and merely confuse me.

HUBERT: It would solve everything, for a little while, and then we could quarrel again later in the day.

CHARLOTTE: No, Hubert.

HUBERT (*taking her in his arms*): Yes, Charlotte.

He kisses her.

CHARLOTTE (*surrendering*): Oh, my love——

HUBERT: Whisper that again.

CHARLOTTE (*almost inaudibly*): Oh, my love.

With his mouth nearly touching hers.

HUBERT: Are you still lost?

CHARLOTTE: Hubert——

HUBERT: Still unhappy?

CHARLOTTE: Please—please——

HUBERT: Come away—come back to the night for a little——

He kisses her again lingeringly and passionately.

They both stand locked in each other's arms oblivious to sight or sound.

SERENA *and* AXEL *come quietly in from the terrace and stand for a moment looking at them.*

SERENA (*breaking the silence*): It is almost time for luncheon, Hubert.

49

HUBERT *and* CHARLOTTE *break away from each other.*
CHARLOTTE *gives a slight scream.*

HUBERT: I find this difficult to forgive, Serena.

SERENA: I am glad to know that we still have something in common.

CHARLOTTE: Axel!

SERENA: There seemed to be no one about in the front of the house so we came round by the terrace.

HUBERT: There is a bell outside the front door, an exceedingly loud bell.

SERENA: To be awakened from a dream by a bell is always disagreeable.

AXEL: Here is your necklace, Mrs. Baxter-Ellis—reset and delivered as you requested by special courier.

CHARLOTTE (*dimly*): Thank you.

HUBERT: Why have you come, Serena?

SERENA: I should have imagined the reason to be fairly obvious.

HUBERT: On the contrary I find it most obscure. What could you possibly hope to achieve by this, this tasteless twofold intrusion?

SERENA: Let us dispense with artificial bluster, Hubert. The situation is both difficult and delicate.

HUBERT: It is also irrevocable.

SERENA (*calmly*): Surely not so irrevocable as to preclude all discussion.

HUBERT: My dear Serena——

SERENA *takes off her gloves.*

SERENA: Please say something, Mr. Diensen. The conversational burden so far has rested almost exclusively on my shoulders. It really is not quite fair.

AXEL: I am at a loss, ma'am, and when I am at a loss all but the crudest phrases elude me.

SERENA: We are all at a loss, which is not surprising in the circumstances. (*To* CHARLOTTE.) Perhaps you would like to speak to your husband privately, Mrs. Diensen?

CHARLOTTE: I have nothing to say to my husband now or at any other time.

SERENA: I hope that you will reconsider that decision later on. Sullen silence is not only unco-operative but extremely irritating. There is a great deal to be discussed. Is there not, Mr. Diensen?

AXEL: There surely is, ma'am.

SERENA: Thank you. That was at least a contribution, if only a minor one.

HUBERT: There is nothing to be discussed, Serena, except by our lawyers. Please understand that once and for all. Even your famous high-handedness cannot transform what is essentially an emotional situation into a debate.

SERENA: As far as I am concerned the situation is not in the least emotional, and I intend to discuss it fully from every angle. That is why we are here, is it not, Mr. Diensen?

AXEL: That is so, ma'am. (*To* HUBERT *and* CHARLOTTE.) This is all hell of a mess and we are here to get it settled one way or another.

HUBERT: It is already settled one way, there is no other.

AXEL: You are a God-damned adulterer, sir.

SERENA: An accurate statement, Mr. Diensen, but over-emphatic. Please remember your promise.

AXEL: I am sorry.

SERENA (*conversationally*): Mr. Diensen promised me on the steamer and again in the train to restrain his temper, Hubert. He is a man of naturally strong feeling; he is also, as you may observe, physically in the pink of condition. I beg of you in your own interest as well as in the interest of general decorum, not to try his patience too far.

HUBERT: I am no more impressed by Mr. Diensen's physical prowess than I am by his uncouth manners.

SERENA: Do remember that, having eloped with Mr. Diensen's wife, you are in no position to criticise his manners. I would be very much obliged if you would pour me out a glass of wine: the journey was hot and dusty and I feel quite exhausted. (*She sits down.*)

There is silence while HUBERT *goes over to a side table upon which is a decanter of wine and some glasses. He pours out some wine and brings it to* SERENA.

HUBERT (*coldly*): A little wine, Mr. Diensen?

AXEL: Thank you. I will help myself.

HUBERT: Do by all means. Charlotte?

CHARLOTTE: No thank you.

AXEL goes to the side table and pours himself a glass of wine.

SERENA: What time is luncheon? I am exceedingly hungry.

HUBERT: You intend to stay to luncheon?

SERENA: We intend to stay indefinitely.

HUBERT: I fear that that is out of the question. There are not enough rooms to begin with, and the domestic staff consists merely of one old woman and her husband and a girl who comes down from the village three times a week to do the cleaning.

SERENA: You seem to forget, Hubert, that I know this villa well. In the earlier, more halcyon days of our married life, we took it for a whole winter. During that

time we managed to put up a number of people includ-
ing that unpleasant nephew of yours who ultimately
had to be sent to the Colonies. There is ample accom-
modation for six guests not counting the room at the
back with the stove in it.

HUBERT: Serena——

SERENA: As for the domestic staff, that is merely a
question of organisation.

HUBERT (*bitterly*): You would reduce the sun and the
moon and the stars in their courses to a question of
organisation.

SERENA: Indeed I would if the Almighty had not so
successfully forestalled me.

AXEL: Bully for you, ma'am.

SERENA: Thank you, Mr. Diensen.

HUBERT: Without wishing to appear inhospitable,
Serena, I fear that I must state firmly and emphatically
that you and Mr. Diensen are *not* going to stay in this
villa indefinitely. You are not even going to stay for
luncheon.

CHARLOTTE: Hubert, I really think——

HUBERT: Hush, my treasure.

SERENA: Considering that that is virtually the only
sound that has emerged from your treasure since our
arrival, it is unkind of you to discourage her.

HUBERT: You have always been a hard and determined woman, Serena.

SERENA: Not quite always. In our earlier years I was
malleable enough but the skies were clear then and the
breezes gentle: later, when the bleak winds of disillusion blew cold, my heart froze a little and my
character suffered a sea change. It was only to be
expected.

HUBERT: What was your object in making this tactless excursion? What could you hope to gain by it?

SERENA (*sipping her wine, rather wearily*): I do not hope to gain anything, Hubert. I cherish no romantic notions of winning you back to me. All I am trying to do is to salvage a little of our mutual dignity.

AXEL: Lady Heronden is perfectly right, Charlotte.

CHARLOTTE (*with spirit*): I am sure she is according to her lights. Apparently she is always perfectly right. Perhaps if she had not been so . . . so frigidly correct for so many years, this situation would never have occurred.

AXEL: Please come out on to the terrace—I wish to speak to you alone.

CHARLOTTE: I have already said that I have nothing to say to you.

AXEL: But I have a great deal to say to you.

HUBERT: Say what you like, Mr. Diensen. Charlotte has given away her heart, I suspect for the first time. It is a gallant, loving, shining heart, untarnished by compromise: none of your plans or arguments can move it now. She has flitted from your self-made world. She will never return.

AXEL: If I had not already been warned about your high-flown phraseology, sir, I should think you were plumb crazy.

HUBERT: You would think so, anyhow. We speak different languages.

AXEL: I have always found the language of common sense sufficient for my needs, and common sense, in this particular instance, has made at least three facts clear to me. The first is that Charlotte is returning to England with me immediately, if I have to carry her there by force; the second is that apart from your noble heritage and your verbal felicity, you are nothing but an irresponsible, frivolous libertine . . .

HUBERT (*angrily*): Now look here, Mr. Diensen . . .

AXEL (*overriding him*): The third fact is that if you are unwise enough to indulge in any further equivocation and fiddle-faddle, it will give me immense pleasure to knock you senseless.

At this moment MR. SPEVIN *appears nervously on the terrace and taps on the shutter. Everybody jumps.*

HUBERT: Good God!

MR. S.: Am I intruding, my lord? There seemed to be no one about in the front of the house so I came round by the terrace.

HUBERT (*recovering himself*): Please come in, Mr. Spevin.

MR. S.: You honour me, my lord, by remembering my name. So kind—so very kind. (*To* CHARLOTTE.) I hope that your ladyship is rested after that long and tedious journey? (*To* AXEL.) We met in the buffet at Boulogne, you know, after a most disagreeable crossing. My little girl was dreadfully seasick, poor mite, but she is now as gay as a cricket.

AXEL: Bully for her.

MR. S. (*puzzled*): I beg your pardon?

HUBERT: Mr. Diensen is an American, Mr. Spevin.

MR. S.: How interesting, how very interesting, the new world, so vital. One of my parishioners is married to an American, from a place called Philadelphia.

AXEL: I have heard of it, sir.

MR. S.: The name is Potter. Perhaps you have run across the family at one time or another?

SERENA (*to* AXEL): You might conceivably have

run over one or two of them, might you not, Mr.
Diensen?

MR. S. (*puzzled again*): I fear that I——

SERENA (*gently*): Mr. Diensen is a railway man and that
was a foolish little joke.

MR. S. (*with an eager smile*): Oh, I see—I see. I will
tell Mrs. Potter. She is a woman of ready humour.

SERENA: My husband has omitted to introduce us.
I am Lady Heronden.

MR. S. (*flustered, darting a look at* CHARLOTTE): Oh,
I—er—I—I'm afraid I——

SERENA: An understandable mistake, Mr. Spevin.
My husband escorted Mrs. Diensen to the buffet at
Boulogne while Mr. Diensen took me directly to the
train. Like your daughter, I too was a little under the
weather.

MR. S.: My wife was quite right after all. She was
positive that—er—Mrs. Diensen was not your ladyship.
We argued about it quite heatedly all the way to
Paris.

SERENA: Perhaps you will take a glass of wine with
us?

MR. S.: No—no—thank you so much—I really must
be getting back. I merely called on the chance of finding
you at home. (*To* HUBERT.) I hope you will forgive the
informality?

HUBERT (*stiffly*): Delighted, Mr. Spevin——

MR. S.: I happened to be passing the house on my
way home from a triste little mission. Poor Lady
Bonnington——

SERENA: Good heavens! Is she still alive?

MR. S.: Oh yes, but alas, her little pug passed over.

SERENA: How sad.

MR. S.: He was very old, of course, but she was devoted to him. She asked me to conduct a brief burial service in the garden. I could hardly refuse, could I? She was so very upset.

HUBERT: I trust that the macaws are still extant?

MR. S.: Oh yes, they attended the service. (*After a slight pause.*) I was wondering if I might ask a small favour? I do so hope that you will not consider it presumptuous on my part, but——

SERENA: What is it, Mr. Spevin?

MR. S. (*with a rush*): One of my parishioners, a Mrs. Edgar Venables, has lent us her garden tomorrow afternoon for a jumble sale in aid of the choir outing. There is to be a raffle and competitions and some quite amusing races. It would give such tremendous cachet to the whole affair if you and his lordship would honour us with your presence and perhaps, I only say perhaps, consent to give the prizes?

HUBERT (*firmly*): Now look here, Mr. Spevin——

MR. S.: It is all on a very small scale of course, nothing grand or distinguished, but it is English. I often describe my little church as an English island in a foreign sea. It means a great deal to me. You do understand, do you not?

SERENA (*decisively*): Of course we do, Mr. Spevin, and we shall be charmed to come to your jumble sale.

HUBERT (*protesting*): Serena——

SERENA: *And* give the prizes. What time would you like us to arrive?

MR. S.: I am quite overwhelmed by your kindness, Lady Heronden. About four-thirty. I think everything will be well under way by then. Do you really mean that you will come?

SERENA: Certainly. We will all come. Will we not, Mr. Diensen?

AXEL: Whatever you say, ma'am.

SERENA: And afterwards you shall show us your "English island in a foreign sea".

MR. S.: I can never express my gratitude, never. My wife will be in the seventh heaven. I can scarcely wait to tell her. Thank you—thank you a thousand times—so kind—so very kind!

MR. SPEVIN, *spluttering with excitement, bows to everyone and goes out via the terrace.*

HUBERT: I have no intention of going to a church jumble sale tomorrow or at any other time. In fact I have no intention of seeing Mr. Spevin ever again in my life. He has already obtruded himself on my privacy twice in thirty-six hours and I have been reasonably civil. That is enough.

SERENA: In that case I shall go alone and make excuses for you. After all it is merely what I have been doing for over twenty years.

HUBERT: Once and for all, Serena, will you kindly leave this house and take Mr. Diensen with you? Your presence here is acutely embarrassing. I regret that you should be inconvenienced, I regret your possible unhappiness. To you too, Mr. Diensen, I tender my most sincere apologies. More than that I cannot say. I cannot even say that I am sorry because the ecstatic beating of my heart would strangle the words in my throat. Come into the garden, Charlotte, this room is suffocating me.

CHARLOTTE: But, Hubert——

AXEL: Stay where you are, Charlotte.

HUBERT (*seizing her by the hand*): Come, my dear love, come out under the sky, away from the dangerous

58

endeavours of those who so implacably wish us well.

HUBERT *takes* CHARLOTTE *out on to the terrace.*

AXEL *makes a movement as if to follow them.* SERENA *sits down again and proceeds to remove her hat.*

SERENA: You are quite content to let them go, Mr. Diensen? Out under the sky?

AXEL: Certainly, ma'am. They'll be back soon. It is beginning to rain.

They look at each other. Then they smile.

THE LIGHTS FADE.

Early the next morning.

 Axel *is seated at the breakfast table. He is thoughtfully sipping a cup of coffee and smoking a cigarette. After a moment or two* Serena *comes in.*

Serena: Good morning, Mr. Diensen.

Axel (*rising*): Oh!—Good morning. (*He is about to crush out his cigarette.*)

Serena: Pray do not stop smoking on my account, I like the smell of tobacco.

Axel: Would you care for some fresh coffee?

Serena: No, thank you, I have already breakfasted in my room. (*She walks over to the window.*) A lovely day, not a cloud, not a breath of wind. We at least have that to be thankful for.

Axel: I trust that you slept well?

Serena: Quite well, thank you, but not enough. Yesterday was a difficult day, it began early and ended very much too late. I feel a little tired.

Axel: You betray no signs of it.

Serena: Thank you, Mr. Diensen.

Axel: May I take this opportunity of saying how profoundly I admire you?

Serena: Thank you again. You are most encouraging.

Axel: Not merely as a woman, that goes without saying, but as an executive.

Serena: You overwhelm me, Mr. Diensen.

AXEL: Your handling of this whole damned business is beyond praise. From the moment we arrived yesterday until the early hours of this morning you have displayed qualities of endurance, patience and determination that Abraham Lincoln would have envied.

SERENA: Mr. Lincoln abolished slavery, I have merely been fighting to re-establish it.

AXEL: There is bitterness in your voice.

SERENA: There is bitterness in my heart, Mr. Diensen.

AXEL: Eliminate it, ma'am, it will stain your shield. This is a trivial adventure.

SERENA: Is it? I wonder.

AXEL: Measured against the world's deeper sorrows of course it is. We must not, even in the interests of self-justification, magnify our comedy into a tragedy. Tragedy inflicts deeper wounds than those we have suffered. Our cause is reasonable enough, I grant you, but it is hardly a crusade, merely an assertion of pride.

SERENA (*with a faint smile*): Bully for you, Mr. Diensen.

AXEL: Are you laughing at me?

SERENA: No more than at myself.

AXEL: A healthy sign at any rate.

SERENA (*turning again to the view*): Do you see that village on the hill?

AXEL (*joining her at the window*): Yes.

SERENA: Just to the right of it, below the little church, there is a clump of cypresses.

AXEL: I see it.

SERENA: It marks an old enclosed garden where the wall has crumbled at one end and you can look out over the olive groves to the sea. Many years ago, when Hubert and I had this house, we escaped from our guests one evening after dinner and drove up there by ourselves in the moonlight. We were much younger then, of course—it was a year before my son died. It was an evening I shall always remember, a special enchantment, detached from everything else. Would it be a healthy sign if I laughed at that too?

AXEL: Perhaps not a guffaw, ma'am, just a grateful smile.

SERENA: Have all American railway magnates so light a touch?

AXEL: Every man jack of them.

SERENA (*coming away from the window*): Do you think we are wasting our time?

AXEL: Maybe, who knows?

SERENA: It was your impulse that brought us here.

AXEL: I accept full responsibility.

SERENA: What spoils will the day yield to us, have you envisaged them?

AXEL: Courage, ma'am.

SERENA: Each of us leading home in triumph a whimpering hostage! Poor pickings, Mr. Diensen.

She turns away.

I do not think that I can face the humiliation.

AXEL: Is your resolution fading?

SERENA: I do not know. I only know that I feel curiously degraded.

AXEL (*vehemently*): This is horrible, horrible!

SERENA: What do you mean?

AXEL: To see you disintegrating before my eyes, crumbling away like the walls of your enchanted garden.

SERENA: Your simile is unattractive.

AXEL: So is this shocking access of weakness in you.

A whiff of memory, a light stab of nostalgia, and down you topple from your pedestal——

SERENA (*tartly*): Please be quiet, Mr. Diensen. You are aggravating me considerably.

AXEL: To think that a few cypress trees could wreak such havoc in so sturdy a heart! It is mortifying.

SERENA: I withdraw my recent implication regarding your lightness of touch. At the moment your misplaced badinage has all the subtlety of a herd of buffalo.

AXEL: That is better.

SERENA (*suddenly very angry*): I refuse to accept your arbitrary decisions as to what is better or worse.

AXEL (*meekly*): As you say, ma'am.

SERENA: But kindly remember that we are still, to all intents and purposes, strangers to each other.

AXEL: Bravo! The stench of powder and the clash of steel!

SERENA: And if you imagine that our present circumstances have, in any way, established a basis of whimsical intimacy between us, I assure you that you are very much mistaken.

AXEL: Stuff and nonsense.

SERENA: I beg your pardon?

AXEL: So you should, Lady Heronden, so you should.

SERENA: Well, really——

AXEL: This damned high horse of yours is a thought too frisky. You mustn't allow him to bolt with you.

SERENA (*icily*): Mr. Diensen——

AXEL: Whereas you undoubtedly have every right to lose control of your temper with your erring husband, you have no right whatsoever to lose it with me.

SERENA: How dare you speak to me like that!

AXEL: Dare Lady Heronden? What do you imagine I have to fear from your intricate high-bred tantrums? So we are still strangers to each other, are we? And any assumption of friendliness, of "whimsical intimacy" on my part must therefore be branded as impertinence. You alone it seems are to have the privilege of deciding our mutual status!

SERENA: Once and for all, Mr. Diensen, I will not be spoken to like this.

AXEL: Stuff and nonsense! I said it once and I say it again. Also poppycock, fiddlesticks, and hell and damnation!

He stamps out on to the terrace.

SERENA *puts her hand out as though to restrain him and then withdraws it and stands looking after him, biting her lip.* CHARLOTTE *enters. She stops short on seeing* SERENA.

CHARLOTTE: Oh!

SERENA: Good morning.

CHARLOTTE (*stiffly*): I am looking for Axel, my husband.

SERENA: I am delighted to hear it.

CHARLOTTE: Do you happen to have seen him?

SERENA: He is in the garden I believe.

CHARLOTTE: Thank you. (*She goes towards the window.*)

SERENA: Just a moment, Mrs. Diensen——

CHARLOTTE (*stopping*): Forgive me, Lady Heronden, but I fear that we have nothing to say to each other.

SERENA: On the contrary, I should think that, taken all in all, we have many mutual interests—by now.

CHARLOTTE: This is an impossible situation and the sooner it is ended the better.

SERENA: I quite agree. That is why I wished to talk to you.

CHARLOTTE: Surely everything has been said that could possibly be said?

SERENA: You mean that a decision has been reached?

CHARLOTTE: No, I do not. I mean that I cannot stand any more. I am near breaking point.

SERENA: Where is Lord Heronden?

CHARLOTTE: I have not the least idea. I have not seen him since—since last night.

SERENA: Please sit down, Mrs. Diensen.

CHARLOTTE: I would rather not.

SERENA: Will you answer me one question?

CHARLOTTE: That depends upon what the question is.

SERENA: Do you really love my husband?

CHARLOTTE: Does it matter to you whether I love him or not?

SERENA (*gently*): Please answer my question. I want, most earnestly, to know the truth.

CHARLOTTE: Why should you concern yourself with that kind of truth? So long as you get your own way, so long as scandal is averted and the situation saved from your point of view, why should it be of the faintest interest to you whether I love Hubert or not?

SERENA: Because, although you may not believe me, his happiness is of great importance to me.

CHARLOTTE (*with a bitter little laugh*): Happiness! Really, Lady Heronden.

SERENA: You must remember that I have been married to him for many years. I know him well.

CHARLOTTE: He is in love with me.

SERENA: I am fully aware of that. He was in love with me once, you know.

CHARLOTTE: A very long time ago.

SERENA: He, however, has been in love several times since. There was a German actress called Lotte Schell; she had large, china-blue eyes and was very sentimental. Then there was a Mrs. Railston; she had an excellent figure but was married, unfortunately, to a card-sharper. I believe they went to South Africa eventually.

CHARLOTTE: There is no necessity for you to give me a list of your husband's mistresses.

SERENA: I think you should at least know their names if only for reference. He is bound to allude to them from time to time. Then there was Hermione Grace——

CHARLOTTE: Lady Heronden——

SERENA (*ignoring her interruption*): She was the widow of an Indian colonel. Hubert was devoted to her for nearly two years. She died ultimately in Harrogate and left him a set of Benares brass-ware, a large luncheon gong and a musical box that played three tunes and had a picture of Loch Lomond inside the lid. I am afraid we still have it somewhere.

CHARLOTTE: What is your object in telling me all this?

SERENA: Merely to prove to you that with Hubert the state of "being in love" is impermanent.

CHARLOTTE: I see.

SERENA: And to discover what, if anything, you have to put in its place when the time comes?

CHARLOTTE: The time may not come. Hubert may continue to be in love with me.

SERENA: Pigs might fly, Mrs. Diensen, but as a general rule they don't.

CHARLOTTE: You have been at some pains to explain

Hubert's fickleness, presumably with the object of frightening me, of making me doubt the genuineness of his feeling for me, but there is one fact that you have overlooked, a very significant fact.

SERENA: And what is that?

CHARLOTTE: He has never, with the other ladies that you mention so glibly, made any personal sacrifices, has he? He has never, for instance, left you before? Never been prepared to jettison his name and position and reputation for any one of them. He has done this for me, Lady Heronden, and there can have been no other reason except that he loved me enough to consider it worth while.

SERENA: Perhaps the others were more foolish than you, or more kind. Perhaps they were willing to accept him on more generous terms.

CHARLOTTE: I do not know what you mean.

SERENA: You are demanding a great deal of him, you know. He will require substantial dividends later on.

CHARLOTTE (*angrily*): And what of his demands of me? I am making the same sacrifices, am I not?

SERENA: No, not quite the same. You have less to lose and more to gain.

CHARLOTTE: And what do you mean by that?

SERENA: If I were willing to divorce Hubert and your husband were willing to divorce you, you could eventually marry Hubert and return to America as the Marchioness of Heronden. It would still be a name of considerable social value even with the shadow of past scandal on it.

CHARLOTTE: You shock me, Lady Heronden. You really do.

SERENA: Don't be silly, Mrs. Diensen.

67

    HUBERT *comes in from the hall.*

Ah, there you are, Hubert. We were wondering what had become of you.

HUBERT: I have been for a long walk.

SERENA: Mrs. Diensen and I have been having a little chat.

HUBERT (*gloomily*): How nice.

CHARLOTTE: It was not nice, it was abominable. I feel defiled.

SERENA: That is natural enough in the circumstances.

CHARLOTTE (*breaking down*): Hubert—what am I to do? Where am I to turn? I can bear no more of this. For heaven's sake take me away, do not let me ever have to speak to her again—I can bear no more—I can bear no more—— (*She bursts into tears.*)

HUBERT (*to* SERENA): There now. You have made her cry again.

SERENA: I claim no credit for that. She has wept at regular intervals from two o'clock yesterday afternoon until the early hours of this morning.

HUBERT: Do you blame her?

SERENA: No, Hubert. I do not blame her. She has every right to cry if she feels like it. I only wish that she would not feel like it quite so often.

HUBERT (*to* CHARLOTTE): My dearest heart, please try to control yourself.

CHARLOTTE: Don't come near me.

    AXEL *comes in from the terrace.*

AXEL: What is happening?

SERENA: Your wife has broken down again.

AXEL: Now see here, Charlotte——

CHARLOTTE: Leave me alone. I do not wish to speak to you. I do not wish to speak to anybody.

AXEL: In that case might I suggest that you go upstairs and lie down? You cannot appear at Mr. Spevin's jumble sale with red eyes.

CHARLOTTE: I am not going upstairs, and I am not going to the jumble sale either.

SERENA: It was agreed last night that we would all go to the jumble sale. Outward appearances at least must be upheld.

CHARLOTTE: I don't care any more what happens.

SERENA: Give her some wine, Mr. Diensen, she is becoming hysterical.

CHARLOTTE (*making a supreme effort and speaking quietly*): I do not want any wine. I want to know what you have decided to do, Hubert. I want to know now.

HUBERT: But, Charlotte——

CHARLOTTE: You have not spoken to me since last night. You have been for a long walk. During that time you must have arrived at some conclusion, made some sort of decision.

HUBERT: You mistrust my love for you. I can hear it in your voice. You are betraying me in your heart. I can feel it! I can feel it!

AXEL: Well, I'll be damned!

SERENA: Please, Mr. Diensen.

CHARLOTTE: Your wife has won, has she not, Hubert? You knew she would from the very beginning; she always has and she always will, is not that the truth? Is it not that that prevented you from speaking to me this morning and sent you off on your lonely walk; the realisation that it was no use fighting any more, that she was too strong for you, that you were bound by all the years of her dominance to give in, to surrender unconditionally, to squirm on the ground with your legs in the air like a beaten, faithful spaniel?

SERENA: An only moderately faithful spaniel.

HUBERT: The conversation has taken an ugly turn. I resent it. Your eyes are suddenly hard, Charlotte. There is a steely note in your voice that I cannot recognise. You are dragging Boston into Arcadia.

AXEL: If this is Arcadia, give me Kansas City.

SERENA: Please be quiet, Mr. Diensen.

CHARLOTTE (*ignoring all interruptions*): Your wife asked me a question a short while ago, a question that I did not answer. She asked me if I really loved you. Well, I answer it now, and the answer is No.

HUBERT (*horrified*): I forbid you to say another word. This is madness!

CHARLOTTE: I believed I loved you with every fibre of my being. I was willing to sacrifice my reputation, to endure social ostracism in order to spend the rest of my life with you, but not now, not any more. The scales have fallen from my eyes, I have seen you in your true colours. They are pale colours, Hubert, and they fade too easily in the glare of conflict. Ever since your wife and my husband arrived in this house yesterday I have watched you twisting and turning, retreating and evading. You have wit and charm and a noble heritage indeed; but your character is watery.

HUBERT: Watery! May God forgive you.

CHARLOTTE (*with dignity*, *to* AXEL): I will return to London with you whenever you wish, Axel. I will also endeavour, in every way I can, to right the wrong I have done you. But please remember one thing, will you? It was not your love that I betrayed, merely your pride. Forgive me, Lady Heronden, for so nearly shattering the admirable façade of your married life. It would have been a cruel thing to do as it is so obviously all you have left.

CHARLOTTE *sweeps out, leaving an uncomfortable silence behind her.*

HUBERT *breaks it.*

HUBERT (*bitterly to* SERENA): I hope you are satisfied.

SERENA: I am far from satisfied.

HUBERT: You have achieved your object. With implacable, fiendish vandalism, you have rent the fabric of romance into a thousand pieces; you have trampled brutally on a dream, stamping it into the ground, mangling it beyond recognition. You have ridden roughshod through my private heart swaggering and looting and burning until there is nothing left but emptiness and desolation. You are not a woman, Serena, you are a Juggernaut. I shall never forgive you for this. Never—never—never until the grave closes over me.

HUBERT *stamps out on to the terrace.*

SERENA (*sits down*): I feel very tired.

AXEL: A little wine?

SERENA: Thank you.

AXEL (*pouring it*): We have won.

SERENA: Yes.

AXEL: I wonder if all victories carry with them such a curious sense of deflation?

SERENA: I expect so.

AXEL (*handing her a glass of wine*): This should be a moment of exultation.

SERENA: I know.

AXEL: It should make this rather acid Red wine taste like champagne.

SERENA (*sipping it*): It still tastes like rather acid Red wine.

AXEL: Have you forgiven me for my boorishness a little while ago?

SERENA: Yes. Have you forgiven me?

AXEL: Yes.

SERENA: And Charlotte, and Hubert?

AXEL: Yes, I suppose so. But I have not forgiven Fate.

SERENA: Why do you say that?

AXEL: Do you not know, Lady Heronden?

SERENA (*firmly*): No. Nor do I wish to. Perhaps after all we were wrong to have come, perhaps it would have been wiser to have let them go.

AXEL: For their sakes or our own?

SERENA: It would at least have been more dignified.

AXEL: Is dignity so all important?

SERENA: Oh yes—yes. To me it is. Vulgarity humiliates me. These last few days have made me so ashamed.

AXEL: And yet vulgarity can be warm, sometimes, warm and lively and human. Dignity on the other hand is cold always. I am surprised that you set such store by it.

SERENA: There are different kinds. Please do not be too hard on dignity; it has much to recommend it.

AXEL: Did he really love Charlotte, do you suppose? Does he really love her?

SERENA: Oh no. It is all a question of degree, of capacity. Hubert has never really loved anybody. Not even me.

AXEL: Then he is a sad and dull man. An insensitive fool.

72

SERENA: I cannot permit you to speak like that of my recently reclaimed husband. It is most unsuitable.

AXEL: He must have loved you, ma'am, in your early married years when you were young together and the privileged world was at your feet, when he was handsome and gay and you were so beautiful.

SERENA: It pains me to have to confess that I was not beautiful, Mr. Diensen. I was gauche and skinny, my legs were too long and my shoulders bony. My eyes were good but alas, on the small side. In later years, however, I am glad to say that I improved.

AXEL: You certainly did.

SERENA: I am grateful for your vehemence. It is most comforting.

AXEL: And he never loved you, this poor lordling?

SERENA: He thought he did. He treated the idea of me most ardently, most tenderly, but it was his idea, not mine. The whole of our life together has been his idea really; I have merely carried it out. Even to coming here and spanking him and putting him in the corner. He relied upon it and expected it in his innermost heart, I am sure he did.

AXEL (*gently*): You had a son and he died?

SERENA: Yes. I had a son and he died.

AXEL: And nothing more? Nothing else—ever?

SERENA: A comfortable and civilised life, Mr. Diensen, and, during the last few years at least, an excellent cook.

AXEL: I congratulate you.

SERENA: Thank you.

At this moment OCTAVIA, COUNTESS OF BONNINGTON, *appears on the terrace. Her age might be anything between sixty and eighty. Her hair is snow white and her skin leathery brown from exposure to the sun. She is wearing a shapeless old russet-coloured tea gown and sandals. She also wears three ropes of valuable pearls and several expensive bracelets. She tiptoes into the room unobserved by* SERENA *and* AXEL. *She scrutinises them carefully through a lorgnette which she carries suspended by a wide black ribbon round her neck.*

OCTAVIA: They were right then, my wild, fervent voices!

AXEL (*turning swiftly*): Good God!

SERENA (*rising hurriedly*): What on earth——?

OCTAVIA: Do not move, either of you. I absolutely forbid it. Stand there where you are, shining with your secret radiance. It is so sweet to see, so very, very sweet.

AXEL: You may not be aware of it but this is a private villa, madame.

OCTAVIA: I know it well. It lies ghostly and empty for long stretches of time, and then suddenly, hey presto! it comes to life again. Lights appear in the windows and smoke curls from the kitchen chimney, which incidentally needs sweeping, and I listen on my hill for the sound of lover's voices.

AXEL: Madame, I really feel that——

OCTAVIA: If I have offended you I apologise. But I was unable to resist the impulse to come. My instincts tugged at me and I had to obey them, I had to see for myself if it was true.

SERENA: I fear there has been some mistake.

OCTAVIA: No mistake. No mistake at all. And I was so afraid that there would be, that they'd lied to me; you know what they are, always prone to over-egg the pudding, always given to exaggeration.

74

AXEL: We have no idea, madame, what you are talking about.

OCTAVIA: Never mind, they were right this time. All is well. Oh, indeed, there is no mistake. Every twitter, every whisper was correct. How happy I am, not only for you but for myself.

SERENA: Who was right? And about what?

OCTAVIA: You are naturally shy and a little bewildered. That is only to be expected, the first vital step is so breath-taking, but once taken there is no return; you will find that the awareness of that is most soothing.

SERENA (*stiffly*): I am the Lady of Heronden.

OCTAVIA: Of course you are, my dear. I recognised you immediately. I knew your mother well in the old days; a lovely creature! So charming in some ways and so excessively disagreeable in others. Is she still alive or has God taken her?

SERENA: She died seventeen years ago.

OCTAVIA: They all go, all my old cronies, rustling away into the shadows like leaves. Do you know that I have outlived forty-three of the girls I was at school with? At moments the realisation of it fills me with splendid elation and then back swings the pendulum and I am plunged in loneliness. My little pug Lancelot died the day before yesterday which was a sad shock, although the end had been clearly in sight for some months. He was nearly fourteen years old, which in doggy language means a very great age indeed. But let us not talk of my troubles, let us talk of you, the gallantry of your magnificent gesture, the gauntlet you have so defiantly flung in the teeth of the world.

AXEL: I hate to disillusion you, madame, but——

OCTAVIA: Pray cast evasion to the wind, let us be

75

utterly frank with each other. I am Octavia, Lady
Bonnington.

SERENA: Ah! I am beginning to understand.

OCTAVIA: But perhaps you would be more likely to
know me by my pen-name, Lucien Snow. There now—
does not that wake an echo?

AXEL: I fear, madame, that——

OCTAVIA: I wrote *The Faraway Lovers, Mariposa, the
Story of an Eager Heart*—Mariposa is the Spanish for
butterfly, you know—and *Tender Was She*. That was the
story of a high-bred English girl who ran off into the
Sahara with a Bedouin. It was banned by all the public
libraries but went into several editions.

SERENA (*firmly*): This is Mr. Diensen, Mr. Axel
Diensen.

OCTAVIA (*scrutinising* AXEL *through her lorgnette*): How
foolish people are, are they not? So determined to get
hold of the wrong ends of sticks. All the villagers near
me have described you as an English "Milor" and you,
my dear—(*she turns to* SERENA)—as petite and blonde
with blue eyes!

SERENA: Lady Bonnington——

OCTAVIA: Do not deny anything I implore you. Do
not attempt to repudiate the lovely flame that has fused
your hungry hearts together. As a matter of fact it
would be waste of time for you even to try. I am an old
woman and my life is nearly done, but I am neither deaf
nor blind. I can still hear the beating of wings, still see
the stars in lover's eyes. I stood on the terrace a moment
ago feeling the vibrations between you, the air tre-
mulous with unspoken longing——

SERENA: Please stop, Lady Bonnington. This is
extremely embarrassing.

OCTAVIA: Embarrassing! What rubbish! You have burnt your bridges as I did once long ago. You have turned your backs on stale modesties and petty conventions. You are now free to plunge laughing into the mountain streams, to ride naked together across the meadows——

AXEL: Just a minute, ma'am——

OCTAVIA (*ignoring him*): This is a land where love is understood and revered and seen in its right perspective. Embarrassing indeed! The word belongs to London and fogs and fusty drawing-rooms; there is no place for it here.

SERENA (*helplessly*): Oh dear—what *are* we to do?

OCTAVIA (*suddenly taking* SERENA'S *hands in hers*): Do not be angry with me, I beg of you, for flashing in upon you like a mad bird.

SERENA: It is not a question of being angry, Lady Bonnington, it is merely that——

OCTAVIA (*sympathetically*): I know—I know—I understand more than you think I do.

SERENA: I am afraid you don't—you see——

OCTAVIA: I have thought about you so much since you arrived. If I go up on to my roof I can see the lights of this villa quite clearly. I have imagined you wandering together in the garden under the stars and standing hand in hand on the terrace gazing out over the sea. It has given me such deep pleasure to think of you here, so near me, starting out together on the loveliest adventure of all. I promise you I will not come again unless you invite me: I make no plea for company for I am well accustomed to being alone. But if you should happen to wander up the hill at any time, the gates of my house are just before you come to the village, on the right: there is a little placard with "Villa La Joie" written on it, a trifle faded I fear, but you cannot possibly miss it. A bientot. Stay true to yourselves and to one another. That is all that really matters.

She waves her hand, goes swiftly out on to the terrace and disappears.

SERENA (*sinking down*): How dreadful that was! How perfectly dreadful!

AXEL (*staring after her*): Poor lady—— Poor old girl.

SERENA (*laughing, a trifle nervously*): She is mad, raving, raving mad.

AXEL (*raising his glass*): I drink to her all the same.

SERENA: Mr. Diensen!

AXEL: I drink to her frantic imagery, to her wild, fervent inner voices, to her dead pug dog and to her kindly, lonely heart.

SERENA: Have you become raving mad also?

AXEL (*putting his glass down with a bang on the table*): Yes, ma'am, I believe I have. So help me God I believe I have!

He walks out of the room slamming the door behind him.

THE LIGHTS FADE.

ACT II: SCENE 3

The Same Evening.

     SERENA, CHARLOTTE, HUBERT *and* AXEL *are sitting about the room drinking coffee. The atmosphere is a trifle strained. They are all in travelling clothes.*

SERENA (*to* CHARLOTTE): More coffee, Mrs. Diensen?

CHARLOTTE (*dimly*): No, thank you.

SERENA (*reminiscently*): Poor Mr. Spevin.

HUBERT: There is no necessity to pity Mr. Spevin. He is absolutely delighted with himself and thanks to your misguided interest in his unpleasant little church, he will probably bore the life out of us indefinitely. We shall be inundated with letters by every post, asking for subscriptions and telling us news of his congregation.

SERENA: We can read them aloud. It will be something to do in the evenings.

AXEL: If I may say so, Lord Heronden, I thought that your speech at the drawing of the raffle ticket was a model of brevity and elegance.

HUBERT (*disagreeably*): Thank you very much.

AXEL: You spoke with such ringing sincerity, and your reference to the church being "An English island in a foreign sea" was so apt that it fully merited the burst of gratifying applause it received.

HUBERT: I find your attempts at humour heavy-handed, Mr. Diensen.

AXEL (*equably*): That is what Charlotte always says.

SERENA: There is no point in continuing to be

disagreeable, Hubert. We cannot sit in dead silence and we might just as well talk about the jumble sale as anything else.

HUBERT: Why the devil doesn't the carriage come?

SERENA: It was not ordered until half-past nine.

HUBERT: I find this situation absolutely intolerable.

SERENA: I quite agree. But it cannot be helped, can it? Therefore the only thing to do is to make the best of it.

HUBERT: Would you care to take a stroll in the garden, Charlotte?

CHARLOTTE: Certainly not, thank you.

SERENA: More coffee, Mr. Diensen?

AXEL: No, thank you, ma'am.

SERENA: Hubert?

HUBERT: No, thank you.

SERENA (*after a long pause*): It will be interesting to discover, when we reach London, how the Tichborne case is progressing. I haven't seen a newspaper for days.

HUBERT: Damn the Tichborne case!

SERENA (*to* CHARLOTTE): I do think that on the whole there has been far too much fuss made over the Shah of Persia's visit, don't you?

CHARLOTTE (*listlessly*): Yes—yes, I suppose so.

SERENA: They have rushed him to the Opera and the Albert Hall and the Abbey, they even took him in the Underground railway to Madame Tussaud's. The poor little man must be exhausted. He was probably impressed though. I don't expect they have them in Persia.

HUBERT: What?

SERENA: Underground railways.

HUBERT: I doubt if they have an Albert Hall either.

SERENA (*persevering*): I wonder if the Lathbury's ball was a success. It took place last night.

HUBERT (*grimly*): Did it?

SERENA: They apparently took an endless amount of trouble over it. Harriet told me that——

HUBERT (*vehemently*): For the love of God have done, Serena. It is no use trying to behave as though nothing has happened. We are all on edge. The very air we breathe is acrid with disillusion and emotional strain and there is no sense in stubbornly making believe that it is not. It is perfectly understood that when we arrive back in London no stain, no blemish shall be allowed to deface the shining, united front we present to our foolish friends. All that is agreed. You are the conqueror: you have dictated the terms of surrender and we, the cringing vanquished, will abide by them. But we are not in London yet; we still have time, a few hours, in which to lick our wounds and prepare our bland and expressionless faces for the parade. Leave us in peace and quiet then for just those few hours. Be merciful in your hideous triumph! Or is that too much to ask?

AXEL (*angrily*): Kindly refrain from using that tone to Lady Heronden in my presence.

HUBERT: Go back to your wild west, Mr. Diensen. Return to your Colonial wigwams! And mind your own business!

HUBERT *stamps out of the room.*

AXEL *makes a movement to follow him but* SERENA, *with a gesture, restrains him.*

SERENA: No brawling, I beg of you, Mr. Diensen. Please sit down.

AXEL: But——

SERENA: My husband has always had an overdeveloped gift for oratory. I believe that when he was young his initiation speech in the House of Lords caused quite a sensation.

AXEL: I'll bet it did.

SERENA: You, as a railway man, will agree I am sure, that all high-powered locomotives must be allowed to let off steam occasionally.

CHARLOTTE (*rising*): If you will excuse me, Lady Heronden, I will retire to my room. I have not quite finished packing my dressing-case.

AXEL (*urgently*): Stay here, Charlotte. Your dressing-case can wait.

CHARLOTTE: I cannot stay here. What Hubert said about the strain is only too true. It is suffocating me.

She goes out hurriedly.

SERENA: Please do not let me keep you here if you wish to follow your wife upstairs, Mr. Diensen.

AXEL: I would like a little more coffee if there is any.

SERENA: There is, but it is not very hot.

AXEL: It will do.

SERENA (*pouring coffee into his cup*): My efforts to ameliorate the situation have been dismally unsuccessful, I fear.

AXEL: You did your best, ma'am.

SERENA: Not quite my best. I can be more subtle than that.

AXEL: I have no doubt of it.

SERENA: Perhaps I did behave a little badly, but I found the temptation irresistible. They both looked so hang-dog.

AXEL: You are a truly remarkable woman.

SERENA: Please smoke a cigarette. Instinct tells me that you are longing to.

82

AXEL: Thank you. It is true that tobacco can be soothing in moments of crisis.

SERENA: There is no longer any crisis. Merely anti-climax.

AXEL (*lighting a cigarette*): Uncomfortable though, however you describe it.

SERENA: Yes, very uncomfortable. I think we must be prepared for certain stresses and strains during the next few months. Our victory was too swift perhaps.

AXEL: I shall always remember this episode, this strange adventure we have shared.

SERENA: I too, Mr. Diensen. (*After a silence.*) You will be returning to America shortly?

AXEL: Yes. I am impatient to be gone. The social life of London that Charlotte so enjoys is to me nothing but a restless vacation. I have only endured it for her sake. I want to get back to work.

SERENA: You have always worked? All your life?

AXEL: Yes, ma'am. It has become a habit like smoking; I cannot give it up. My father was an engineer on the early railroads. He drove trains in the dangerous years, through Indian ambushes and storms and blizzards and droughts. We lived in a little village in Illinois which is now a thriving town. I started work when I was thirteen.

SERENA: Thirteen?

AXEL: I was a news-butcher!

SERENA: What is that?

AXEL: A cheeky, shrill-voiced little boy who prances through the rolling trains selling newspapers and questionable magazines and pea-nuts and chewing-tobacco. I learned the facts of life early. Later, of course,

I rose from the ranks, but those first years were useful. I was a fairly bright lad, ma'am.

SERENA (*with a smile*): I would never doubt that for an instant, Mr. Diensen.

AXEL: I worked on freight trains, passenger trains and cattle trains. To me the future always lay at the end of a line. The Iron Horse was my Godhead; as cruel and unpredictable as any of the Gods of Antiquity. He dragged me back and forth across the prairies and deserts and mountains of my country. He took my father from me and two of my brothers. He also, more benevolently, disposed of an uncle in Wisconsin who left me eighteen thousand dollars in his will. That was the beginning of fortune. It seemed to me then as it seems to me now that the destiny of America lies in the increasing power and expansion of her railroads—the annihilation of distance—the drawing together of isolated peoples—the——— (*he breaks off.*) I am boring you. This is my hobby horse, my iron hobby horse. You must not encourage me.

SERENA: Please go on, Mr. Diensen.

AXEL: You are kind, very kind.

SERENA: I am interested.

AXEL: That is kinder still.

SERENA: Pray continue.

AXEL: There is so much that I would like to say to you but my intention falters.

SERENA: Why should it?

AXEL: I envy your husband his gift of words. To you, whose ears are attuned to so much glittering hyperbole, my homespun, rough-shod phrases must sound sadly uninspired.

SERENA: Come, come, Mr. Diensen, this continual

harping on your verbal inadequacy comes perilously near affectation. I am not entirely imperceptive and although our acquaintanceship has been brief I have already suspected that your far-away railroads provided you with ample opportunities for reading.

AXEL: You have seen through me, ma'am. Your sharp mind has unmasked my pitiful little secret.

SERENA: Nonsense, Mr. Diensen. You are too assured to cherish pitiful secrets.

AXEL: Assured! Why, at this very moment the ground is shaking beneath my feet. You are undermining the very foundations of my character.

SERENA: Such exaggeration rings false, but I presume you meant it to.

AXEL: Come to my country one day, ma'am. Your own true quality would immediately recognise its valour and forgive its young vulgarities. It is a great territory, still untamed and rich with promise; even richer in variety. From the white frame houses of New England to the Florida swamps; from the painted streets of Charleston to the adobe villages of California there is so much diversity, so much to fire your imagination. Oh, Lord, the whole of life seems newly washed, seen from the open door of a caboose.

SERENA: Caboose?

AXEL: The tail end of a freight train, the last car of all, a small shaky cabin with a twisted iron ladder climbing to the roof, that is the home of the brakeman. There he sits, hour in hour out, watching the trees marching along and the cinders and earth and sands of America slipping away beneath the wheels. He can watch the sun set over the gentle farmlands of Wisconsin and rise over the interminable prairies of Nebraska and Illinois and Kansas. Those flat, flat lands bring the sky so low that on clear nights you can almost feel that you are rattling along through the stars. It is rougher going in the mountains where there are sharp curves and steep gradients and the locomotive strains and gasps and fills the air with steam and sparks; tunnels close round you, infernos of noise and sulphurous smoke, then suddenly you are in the open and can breathe again and there are snow-covered peaks towering above you and pine forests and the sound of waterfalls. Over it all and through it all, the familiar, reassuring noise of the train; a steady beat on the level stretches when the wheels click over the joints in the rails but changing into wilder rhythms when you clatter over bridges and crossings and intersections. The railroad is my dream, ma'am, the whole meaning of my life, my pride and all my hopes for the future—come to my country one day. Let me take you in a private car from Chicago to the West, a car specially designed by George Mortimer Pullman. The luxury of it will soothe and startle you; sofas and chairs of damask of the most violent patterns but infinitely comfortable; dark, grinning servants to wait on you; fresh iced celery from Kalamazoo. Rainbow trout from the Rocky Mountains, and outside the wide windows of your drawing-room you shall see the New World passing by. . . .

SERENA: I will remember your invitation, Mr. Diensen, even though my circumstances may never allow me to accept it. I will also remember . . . (*She stops abruptly and turns away.*)

AXEL: What is it that you were about to say? What made you stop short so suddenly?

SERENA: It was of no consequence.

86

AXEL: Please do not withdraw, Lady Heronden. It seemed to me that perhaps, at last, we were becoming friends.

SERENA: We will always be friends, Mr. Diensen.

AXEL: Do you mean that, ma'am?

SERENA: Yes, I do.

AXEL (*looking at her*): The carriage will be here at any moment now.

SERENA: I know.

AXEL: Good-bye, Lady Heronden.

SERENA: Good-bye, Mr. Diensen.

She puts out her hand. He bends down and kisses it, then he goes over to the window and stands looking out at the stars with his back to her. HUBERT *comes in wearing an overcoat and hat.*

HUBERT: Francoise and Jean have gone on in the wagonette with the luggage. The carriage is waiting.

AXEL: Where is Charlotte?

HUBERT: She is waiting too. It is time to go.

SERENA (*rising*): Very well.

HUBERT: I think you both might have the grace to look a little more cheerful in your triumph; the atmosphere is full of regrets.

SERENA: I am not feeling particularly triumphant, Hubert.

HUBERT: You should, my dear, you really should. You have got your own way. But then you always do, don't you!

He goes out.

SERENA (*as he goes*): Not quite always. Come, Mr. Diensen.

SERENA *sweeps out followed by* AXEL *as*
THE CURTAIN FALLS.

ACT III: Scene 1

A year later.

Serena's *sitting-room in Heronden House, Belgrave Square.*

> *When the curtain rises, the french windows are wide open, warm afternoon sunlight is flooding into the room and a hurdy-gurdy is playing outside in the square.*
>
> Serena *is seated at her escritoire writing a letter. Occasionally she pauses to think of a word. Suddenly she rises and goes swiftly to the window; she fumbles in her reticule for some coins, then throws them to the organ-grinder and waves her hand gaily. She returns to her letter smiling, adds a couple of words to it and is sealing it up when* Hubert *comes into the room. She gives a slight start and slips the letter into her bag.*

Hubert: Ah—there you are, my dear.

Serena: You say that as though you expected me to be somewhere else. I am usually here at this time of day.

Hubert (*absently*): Yes—yes, I know you are. (*He wanders over to the windows.*) Those damned street organs should not be allowed.

Serena: On the contrary I think they should be encouraged.

Hubert: In heaven's name why?

Serena: The sound has a certain charm.

Hubert: I find little charm in being unable to hear myself speak.

SERENA: I can well understand that, my dear, but on the whole you contrive to hear yourself speak a great deal more than most people.

HUBERT: Charm indeed! The ghastly instrument is out of tune.

SERENA: Perhaps it is but that is part of its appeal. A muffin bell also is out of tune, even the cry of a lavender seller may not be vocally accurate but there is a sweetness in it, an evocative quality. London would be sad without her gentle noises.

HUBERT: Stuff and nonsense!

SERENA: Poppycock! Fiddle-faddle! and hell and damnation! (*She laughs.*)

HUBERT (*startled*): Serena!

SERENA (*meekly*): Yes, Hubert?

HUBERT: What on earth is the matter with you?

SERENA: Nothing, nothing at all.

HUBERT: You seem to be in a strange mood.

SERENA: You also are in a strange mood, more irascible, less cheerful than mine. Has anything happened to upset you?

HUBERT (*shortly*): No.

SERENA: You lunched with poor Roderick?

HUBERT: Yes.

SERENA: He generally amuses you.

HUBERT: Well, he didn't today.

SERENA: Poor Roderick.

HUBERT: Why do you always say "Poor Roderick"?

SERENA: There is something in his determined buoyancy that commands my pity.

HUBERT: He has everything that his heart could desire.

SERENA: Perhaps that is why.

HUBERT: Wit, money, good looks, an understanding wife——

SERENA: I detect a sting of envy in your voice. Do you find me obtuse?

HUBERT: No, Serena. I most certainly do not.

SERENA: Would you say that, on the whole, our marriage had been a success?

HUBERT: What an extraordinary question!

SERENA: Leaving aside the unfortunate episode of last year, would you say, all things considered, that our long years together had been reasonably happy?

HUBERT: Of course I would.

SERENA (*lightly*): It's not quite enough, is it?

HUBERT: What on earth do you mean?

SERENA: "Till death do us part". I have always thought that that particular phrase was didactic and a trifle ingenuous. Life provides so many reasons for parting, death only one.

HUBERT: What is in your mind, Serena? What has prompted this abrupt soul-searching?

SERENA: Hardly soul-searching, merely a light, introspective summing-up.

HUBERT: Summing-up of what?

SERENA: Debits and credits, gains and losses. Surely all well-conducted businesses lay aside a certain time each year for stock-taking?

HUBERT: And how do you find that we stand at the moment? How are our securities?

SERENA (*gaily*): Gilt-edged, Hubert, a trifle static but wonderfully gilt-edged.

HUBERT: Splendid.

SERENA: Yes, it is, isn't it?

HUBERT: You are leaving for Heronden this evening?

SERENA: Yes, on the seven-fifteen train.

HUBERT: I presume that Alford knows?

SERENA: Yes, he is meeting me with the dog-cart at Deal.

HUBERT: Why the dog-cart? It will be dark by the time you arrive.

SERENA: There is a moon tonight, a full moon, didn't you know? The sea will be calm and I shall be able to see the lights on the French coast, so near, so very near.

HUBERT: There may be a fog, or at least a heavy sea mist. There frequently is at this time of year.

SERENA: There won't be tonight.

HUBERT: I am willing to admit that you are a brilliant organiser, Serena, but surely even you must stop short at arranging the climate.

SERENA: I am so glad that you think I have been efficient. You would give me a kind reference, wouldn't you, if you had to? Honest, sober, industrious and——

HUBERT: What *are* you talking about?

SERENA: I am not sure that I know.

HUBERT: I am afraid I shall not be able to get down before Saturday. I have to dine with that fellow Mallory on Friday.

SERENA: Which fellow Mallory?

HUBERT: You know perfectly well. I told you about him last week. He is an Irishman.

SERENA: How delightful.

HUBERT: He is also a first-class shot.

SERENA: The Irish nearly always are, aren't they? I suppose they have to be.

HUBERT: That is what I wanted to talk to you about.

SERENA: Shooting?

HUBERT: No, Mallory.

SERENA: Oh.

HUBERT: I have decided to go to East Africa with him.

SERENA (*astonished*): Hubert!

HUBERT: He is a professional big-game hunter; he is organising an expedition into the interior, and has invited me to join it.

SERENA: Do you really think you will enjoy that?

HUBERT: Why on earth shouldn't I?

SERENA: You have always been so careful of your creature comforts. I find it difficult to imagine you charging through tropical jungles with a gun.

HUBERT: You don't hunt big game in tropical jungles.

SERENA: Nonsense, my dear, of course you do. I was reading about it in Blackwood's. There are swarms of insects and deadly snakes and the air is so stifling that you gasp for breath. I should think you would positively loathe it. When I remember the fuss you made about the heat at Lords only last week——

HUBERT: I am leaving at the end of the month.

SERENA: I see. How long will you be gone?

HUBERT: I am not sure. Six months at least.

SERENA: So it is all decided.

HUBERT: Yes. (*There is a pause.*) Do you mind?

SERENA (*absently*): No—no, Hubert. I don't mind. Why should I?

HUBERT (*apologetically*): I had to say definitely whether I would go or not. Mallory has to plan the whole business and there isn't much time.

SERENA: Will it be a large expedition?

HUBERT: About a dozen all told, I believe.

SERENA: Anyone you know?

HUBERT: No, I don't think so.

SERENA: And you like this man Mallory well enough to spend six months in his company?

HUBERT: He is an engaging fellow. Occasionally witty and always agreeable; and there will be the others.

SERENA (*turning away*): Yes, yes, of course there will.

HUBERT: Are you angry?

SERENA: No, not in the least.

HUBERT: It was perhaps inconsiderate of me to decide to go without consulting you.

SERENA: Were you afraid that I might raise objections? Put difficulties in the way?

HUBERT: No, not exactly. I expect I was a little afraid that you might laugh me out of it.

SERENA: Poor Hubert.

HUBERT: Why do you say that?

SERENA: Chained to a dragon.

HUBERT: You over-dramatise yourself, my love. You are no dragon; merely a woman of extreme sensibility who has become suddenly bored with her own social rectitude. Poor Serena.

SERENA: How perceptive you are!

HUBERT: I regard you, my dear, with the most fearful respect.

SERENA: Tempered, I hope, with at least a residue of affection?

HUBERT: Will you miss me when I have gone?

SERENA: I have missed you for years.

CATCHPOLE *enters*.

CATCHPOLE (*announcing*): Lady Harriet Ripley.

HARRIET RIPLEY *comes in*.

SERENA: My dear Harriet! (*They kiss.*) Bring the tea, will you, Catchpole?

CATCHPOLE: Very good, milady.

He goes out.

HARRIET: How are you, Hubert? (*She shakes hands with him.*)

HUBERT: Well, thank you, Harriet, monotonously well.

HARRIET: Well, that is more than I am—this heat is completely exhausting me. You must be longing to get down to Heronden, Serena.

SERENA: I am, indeed.

HARRIET (*sitting down and proceeding to take off her gloves*): I hear that you had luncheon with poor Roderick today, Hubert. How is he?

HUBERT: Poor Roderick has just made eight thousand pounds on the Stock Exchange, his horse, Tantivy, has won four races in three weeks, and his mother-in-law returned to Argyllshire yesterday.

HARRIET: No wonder Elise looked so excitable at the Royal Academy this afternoon. She was talking at the top of her voice and darting from picture to picture like a bluebottle. She *does* wear the most ramshackle hats, does she not? You would think with all her money that she *might* make a little more effort, wouldn't you?

CATCHPOLE *and a footman enter with the tea-things.*

Ah, here is tea—thank heaven! I am quite prostrate.

SERENA: Are you dining in, Hubert?

HUBERT: No, I am meeting Harry at Boodles' at six o'clock. I must go and change.

SERENA: Surely you will have a cup of tea first?

HUBERT: No, my love. I detest tea and I am sure you and Harriet have much to gossip about.

SERENA: Indeed we have. I feel, Harriet, that you should be the first to know that Hubert is leaving me.

94

HARRIET: Serena!

SERENA: He is going to hunt big game in Africa.

HARRIET: Good gracious! Will you like that, Hubert?

HUBERT: Of course I shall. Why shouldn't I?

HARRIET: It seems so unlike you somehow. I cannot imagine you stalking solemnly for days and days across the African veldt.

HUBERT: I am not going anywhere near the African veldt.

HARRIET: But you of all people! You who set such store by the luxuries of life——

HUBERT (*exasperated*): Both you and Serena seem to regard me as a sort of spineless sybarite, an ageing ninny who is afraid of getting his feet wet. Let me hasten to assure you that you are both entirely mistaken. I am sick and tired of this stuffy insular groove in which I have been stuck fast for years. I long with all my heart and soul to get out into the open for a little; to lie under the stars by a flickering camp-fire, to fill my lungs with fresher, cleaner air, to rest my eyes on new and strange horizons.

HARRIET: Well, at any rate I hope the weather will be nice.

HUBERT: The weather will *not* be nice, Harriet. It may be violent and unpredictable, it may be hot, cold, dry and wet to excess, but it will never, *never* be nice!

By this time CATCHPOLE *and the footman have arranged the tea-table—and withdrawn from the room.*

SERENA: There is no occasion to bellow at Harriet, my dear. She was merely wishing you well.

HUBERT: I know she was, Serena. I am quite sure that you both wish me well, but I would be more appreciative

95

of your well-wishing if it were neither pitying nor patronising. Up to now, it has been both. As I shall probably not see you again before you leave for the station, I will say good-bye now.

SERENA: Very well, dear.

HUBERT: Good-bye for the moment, Harriet.

HARRIET: Good-bye, Hubert. I still hope that you will not live to regret this rather bizarre enterprise.

HUBERT (*ignoring her*): You may expect me on Saturday, Serena.

SERENA (*returning from far away*): Saturday? Oh, yes—of course—Saturday.

HUBERT: Tell Alford to meet me with the trap. I will arrive on the two-thirty from Cannon Street.

SERENA: Yes, Hubert.

HUBERT: And if Hannibal's foot has shown no signs of improvement you had better send for the vet.

SERENA: Yes, Hubert.

HUBERT: That is all, I think, except for Wilcox and his damned thistles, but I will deal with him myself.

SERENA: Yes, Hubert.

HUBERT: Good-bye, Serena. (*He turns to go.*)

SERENA (*with a sudden note of urgency in her voice*): Oh, Hubert——

HUBERT (*turning back*): What is it?

SERENA: It is only that I do wish you well, Hubert, neither pityingly nor patronisingly, but with all my heart—truly I do.

HUBERT (*surprised*): Why—Serena——?

SERENA: Good-bye, Hubert. (*She rises quickly and kisses him on the cheek.*)

HUBERT *goes out—and she returns to the tea table.*

HARRIET: You look flushed.

SERENA: Flushed?

HARRIET: Almost as though you were feverish.

SERENA: I think I am a little feverish.

HARRIET: My dear!

SERENA: Do not be alarmed. It is a mental state more than a physical one.

HARRIET: Why? What has caused it?

SERENA (*laughing*): I have not the remotest idea. Is not that extraordinary?

HARRIET (*suspiciously*): Most extraordinary.

SERENA: Perhaps it is something to do with the climate.

HARRIET: Has anything happened? Anything disturbing?

SERENA: No, I can't think of anything. I saw Mr. Disraeli driving along the Mall this morning. He looked a trifle yellow I thought, but it didn't disturb me at all. After all he has looked fairly yellow for years, has he not?

HARRIET: Never mind about Mr. Disraeli for the moment.

SERENA: Of course I did wave to him which I would never have done to Mr. Gladstone.

HARRIET: Where did you have luncheon?

SERENA: With Etta in Kensington. Ronald and Elizabeth were there, and that moist young man from the German Embassy whose name I can never remember.

HARRIET: Gerhardt von Spiegal, I expect. He always goes everywhere.

SERENA: I cannot imagine why, can you?

HARRIET: He is supposed to be very intelligent.

SERENA: He betrayed no tell-tale signs of it at

97

luncheon. All he did was to eat a great deal and discuss the Princess of Wales's fringe.

HARRIET: Go on.

SERENA: At three o'clock I met Alice at Peter Robinson's and stood by in mute dismay while she chose the most hideous curtain material. Perhaps that is what sent my temperature up! Then I came home, and Miss Francis arrived to do my nails. That is all, really.

HARRIET: I must say I do not know what we should all do without Miss Francis.

SERENA: She is certainly an excellent manicurist.

HARRIET: She is also a positive mine of information.

SERENA (*a little coldly*): Is she indeed?

HARRIET: Did she say anything about that rumpus at the Massinghams'?

SERENA: No.

HARRIET: You should have asked her. It is a fascinating story.

SERENA: I do not encourage Miss Francis to gossip.

HARRIET: Then you should, my dear, you miss a great deal.

SERENA: You really are incorrigible, Harriet.

HARRIET: She can be very entertaining if she chooses. After all, most of our friends employ her.

SERENA: Unwisely, it would seem.

HARRIET: It was she who first told me about the Diensens last year.

SERENA (*looking up*): The Diensens?

HARRIET: She, Mrs. Diensen, ran off, you know, to the south of France with a man called Baxter-Ellis, and her husband had to go and fetch her back. I believe there were the most appalling scenes, but it was all hushed up.

SERENA: And how did the redoubtable Miss Francis find out about it?

HARRIET: Through Mrs. Diensen's maid, apparently. Do you mean to say you didn't know?

SERENA: No. I am singularly innocent about that kind of thing. I always understood that they were a devoted couple.

HARRIET: But you saw quite a lot of them. You must have guessed that something was amiss?

SERENA: They dined here once or twice, that is all.

HARRIET: If you ask me, I think *he* is a bit of a dark horse.

SERENA (*dreamily*): A dark Iron Horse.

HARRIET: What did you say?

SERENA: Nothing.

HARRIET: He is back in England, you know, without her!

SERENA: Is he really?

HARRIET: Violet Trevor saw him at Kew Gardens last week, with a mysterious woman.

SERENA: Heavily veiled, I trust?

HARRIET: As a matter of fact, I believe she was.

SERENA: Toast?

She hands her the hot dish.

HARRIET: No, thank you.

SERENA: That chocolate cake comes from Buszard's. It is quite delicious.

HARRIET (*shaking her head*): According to Miss Francis they are actually in process of being divorced. She is living in Boston with her family while it is all arranged.

SERENA: How wise.

HARRIET: Personally my sympathies are with her. I always found him rather a bore, didn't you?

SERENA: Deadly.

HARRIET: I have come to the conclusion that I detest rugged characters.

SERENA: They can be disconcerting.

HARRIET: Did Hubert like him?

SERENA: Immensely. They used to go for long walks together.

HARRIET: Long walks?

SERENA: Hubert has always been fascinated by trains, you know. I remember him talking a great deal about them on our honeymoon. Of course the whole industry has made vast strides since then and Mr. Diensen was able to bring him up to date as it were.

HARRIET: I see.

SERENA: We really should try to learn more about railways, they so often bring out the best in a man.

HARRIET: How can you be so ridiculous!

SERENA: Would you like some more tea?

HARRIET: No, thank you. (*After a slight pause.*) Will you mind Hubert going to Africa?

SERENA: We must ask Miss Francis, she will be bound to know.

HARRIET: No, but seriously, do you?

SERENA: Of course not.

HARRIET: It was rather a sudden decision, wasn't it?

SERENA: I believe that he has had the idea in his mind for some time. I am sure that it will do him a great deal of good. Take him out of himself.

HARRIET: It will also take him out of harm's way.

SERENA: Harm's way?

HARRIET: It is no use pretending that you don't know what I mean.

SERENA: I am not pretending. I have not the least idea what you mean.

HARRIET (*with a little laugh*): Really, Serena!

SERENA: What are you hinting at, Harriet?

HARRIET: Hubert has a new "friend".

SERENA: That does not surprise me. He is naturally gregarious.

HARRIET: This one is brunette and very vivacious. I am told that she has a charming singing voice, untrained, you know, but absolutely true.

SERENA: Hubert often pretends to have an ear for music, but he hasn't really, so it won't matter much whether her voice is true or not.

HARRIET: Do you seriously mean to tell me that you know nothing about Hubert and this Mrs. Mallory?

SERENA (*sharply*): Mrs. what?

HARRIET: Mallory. She is Irish, so is her husband. Apparently they are rather rolling stones, always travelling about the world. Charles Barrington met them in Egypt last year. I don't think he formed a very favourable impression of them.

SERENA: Why?

HARRIET: It seems that he, Mr. Mallory, is none too scrupulous over money matters.

SERENA: And the wife? Is she unscrupulous too?

HARRIET: Very, I believe.

SERENA: Oh, poor Hubert!

HARRIET: That is what I meant when I said that the trip to Africa would take him out of harm's way.

SERENA: I see it all now.

HARRIET: Is he leaving soon?

SERENA: Yes, at the end of the month.

HARRIET: That should be a great relief to you.

SERENA (*laughing*): It is! Oh, it is!

HARRIET: Why are you laughing?

SERENA: Because I feel gay. I have felt gay all day.

HARRIET: You are certainly in a very strange mood.

SERENA: Hubert said that only a little while ago. I was listening to a hurdy-gurdy playing in the Square, and all at once everything seemed to be vibrant and sweet and full of furtive excitements.

HARRIET: Furtive excitements? What *do* you mean?

SERENA: If he had come into the room a moment later he would probably have discovered me hopping about the floor kicking my legs in the air like a ballet dancer.

HARRIET (*slightly scandalised*): Serena!

SERENA: How do I look, Harriet? Tell me—be a mirror and tell me true. From where you are sitting can you see any crow's feet, any wrinkles?

HARRIET: How absurd you are. Of course I can't.

SERENA: But if I bend closer, there—like that. (*She bends towards* HARRIET.) Now—how do I look?

HARRIET: Candidly, my dear, you look unbalanced.

SERENA: That does not matter. It is the texture that counts. My skin is still soft, is it not? Soft enough at any rate.

HARRIET (*sternly*): Soft enough for *what*, Serena?

SERENA: Soft enough to compensate a little for the hardness of my character.

HARRIET: What rubbish you talk.

SERENA: Do you think there is still time? Do you think it is not too late?

HARRIET: Something must have happened to make you behave like this. What is it?

SERENA: The hurdy-gurdy, perhaps; or the sudden vision I had of poor Hubert filing away so diligently at his chains.

HARRIET: Chains?

SERENA: The stubborn romantic, the eternal troubador, still eager to sing his lilting ballads to anyone who will listen. Oh, how dull I have been to him! And how cruel! Have some bread and butter.

HARRIET: I do not want any bread and butter. I only want to know what has happened to you.

SERENA: Nothing, Harriet, I promise you. Nothing at all.

HARRIET: But why should you suddenly accuse yourself of being cruel to Hubert, when you know perfectly well that but for your amazing patience and tolerance your married life would have broken up years ago?

SERENA: Would the world have come to an end if it had?

HARRIET: No. The world wouldn't have come to an end, but it might have laughed at you, and that would have been intolerable to your pride.

SERENA: How right you are, Harriet. And what a terrible indictment!

HARRIET: Indictment?

SERENA: Yes—oh, dear me, yes! To deny the spring of the year for fear of mockery! What a fool I have been.

HARRIET: Spring of the year, indeed! What nonsense! Hubert is a middle-aged philanderer and old enough to know better.

SERENA: Charm is independent of age. He will always have charm.

HARRIET (*searchingly*): Do you still love him?

SERENA (*with a smile*): Yes. I think that for the first time, I love him enough.

HARRIET: And what can you possibly mean by that?

SERENA: What a becoming hat, Harriet. Is it new?

HARRIET: There are moments when I could willingly slap you, Serena.

SERENA: Dear Harriet. Are you quite sure you won't have some more tea?

HARRIET: You infuriate me, and what is more, you do it deliberately.

SERENA: Just half a cup?

HARRIET (*rising*): No, thank you. I have to go.

SERENA: Tell me more about Mrs. Mallory.

HARRIET: I have told you all I know.

SERENA: Tell me other things, then. Tell me more about Miss Francis. She fascinates me. I see her suddenly in a new light; a refined, suburban truffle-pig, burrowing her way into her clients' confidences, unearthing their sad little secrets, polishing them up to a nice shine, and then selling them round the town.

HARRIET: Miss Francis is a perfectly respectable, hard-working woman, and she earns her living honestly.

SERENA (*with finality*): Good-bye, Harriet.

HARRIET (*startled*): Serena! What do you mean?

SERENA: You said you were going, and I said good-bye. What is there odd about that?

HARRIET: You said it so abruptly.

SERENA: I wish I could make amends.

HARRIET: What for?

SERENA: For being so—so unsatisfactory. We have been friends for so many, many years, and I have given you so little. Dear Harriet!

HARRIET: Good heavens! There are tears in your eyes!

SERENA (*smiling*): I know.

HARRIET: You *are* unhappy about something. I knew it!

SERENA: No, no. On the contrary, I am very happy indeed. (*She unpins a brooch from her gown.*) I want you to have this. (*She holds it out to her.*)

HARRIET (*astounded*): Serena!

SERENA: It belonged to my great-great-great-grandmother. I believe she was very skittish.

HARRIET: But why should you suddenly wish to give it to me?

SERENA: To remember me by.

HARRIET: Are you going away?

SERENA: Yes. The seven-fifteen from Cannon Street. Alford is meeting me at Deal with the dog-cart. I am devoted to Alford, but he is getting dreadfully old. It is very sad, is it not, when people get dreadfully old—so soon? Please take the brooch.

HARRIET (*taking it*): It is exquisite—I hardly know what to say. (*She kisses her.*) Thank you, Serena—I shall treasure it always.

SERENA: That is what I wanted you to say.

HARRIET: You are sure that you are quite well? That there is nothing wrong?

SERENA: Quite, quite sure.

HARRIET (*still puzzled*): Good-bye, my dear.

SERENA: Good-bye, Harriet.

HARRIET *goes out.*

SERENA *stands looking after her for a moment, then she goes over to the bell-rope and pulls it.*

The hurdy-gurdy starts to play again a few streets away. SERENA *smiles and begins to waltz slowly round the room.*

CATCHPOLE *enters.*

CATCHPOLE: You rang, milady?

SERENA (*stopping her dance*): Yes, Catchpole. Has his lordship gone to the club?

CATCHPOLE: He left a few minutes ago, milady.

SERENA (*producing from her bag the letter she was writing at the beginning of the scene*): Will you give him this when he comes in tonight? I shall be gone, and it is rather urgent.

CATCHPOLE (*taking it*): Very good, milady. Will that be all?

SERENA: Yes, Catchpole. That will be all.

CATCHPOLE *goes out and closes the door behind him.*

SERENA *begins to dance again as the lights fade on the scene.*

ACT III: Scene 2

The Buffet de la Gare, Boulogne.

> *The scene is the same as in Act I, Scene 1. Various travellers are seated at various tables, the waiters are scurrying about, and the dawn is grey outside the windows.*

> *At a table downstage* Mr. *and* Mrs. Spevin *and* Gwendolyn *are seated.*

Mr. S.: If it is labelled, the porter will be sure to find it.

Mrs. S.: The label might have come off.

Mr. S.: I understood you to say that you had tied it on firmly. In that case it will not come off.

Gwen: Mama——

Mrs. S.: Be quiet, Gwendolyn, and drink up your tea.

Gwen: If I do, I shall be sick again.

Mr. S.: Try not to think about it.

Mrs. S.: There is no need to snap at the child!

Mr. S.: I did not snap at her. I merely suggested that she might concentrate on something else for a change. (*To* Gwendolyn.) Where is your nice book, dear?

Gwen: In the pilgrim-basket—the one that's lost.

Mr. S.: We have no proof that the pilgrim-basket is lost, Gwendolyn.

Gwen: Mama says it is.

Mr. S.: Even your mama has been known to make mistakes occasionally.

Mrs. S.: Has she indeed?

MR. S.: I happened to see the porter take it out of the train with my own eyes.

MRS. S.: So did I. But I haven't seen it since.

MR. S.: For heaven's sake stop fussing, Sarah!

MRS. S. (*bridling*): Fussing, indeed! I like that, I must say! All Gwennie's things are in that basket; her two summer dresses, her dancing shoes, all her underclothes, to say nothing of her books and her precious pencil box, and all you do is to sit there guzzling tea.

MR. S. (*with admirable control*): I am not *guzzling* tea, Sarah, any more than you are. I am sipping it in a perfectly ordinary manner.

MRS. S.: You ought not to be sipping anything until the luggage is safely on board. Here am I at my wits' end with Gwennie being sick one minute and having hiccups the next, and you just go on behaving as though nothing had happened. Why don't you at least go and look for the porter?

MR. S.: Because I shouldn't be able to find him if I did. He agreed to meet us with the luggage on the lee side of the funnel in half an hour's time. That was ten minutes ago. If the pilgrim-basket isn't there, we will send him to look for it. The boat doesn't sail for ages yet.

MRS. S.: Downright carelessness, that's all it is——

MR. S. (*with sudden firmness*): If you have finished your tea and Gwennie will not drink hers, you had better both go on board and leave me in peace.

MRS. S. (*outraged*): Well, really——!

MR. S.: Here are your tickets. (*He planks down two tickets on the table.*) If you take my advice you will find two chairs on the upper deck and sit in them. I shall stay here and read my newspaper.

MRS. S.: Of all the selfish, inconsiderate . . .

MR. S.: Do as I say, Sarah. I will join you later. And if the basket is lost, it is lost, and as far as I am concerned, good riddance to it!

With a snort of rage MRS. SPEVIN *snatches up the tickets from the table, grabs* GWENDOLYN *by the hand—and churns away with her.*

MR. SPEVIN *opens a French newspaper and settles himself to read it with a sigh of relief.*

A COURIER *comes in, followed by* SERENA *and* AXEL. *He leads them to a table, the same table at which* HUBERT *and* CHARLOTTE *were sitting in the first scene.*

COURIER: This is your reserved table, sir.

AXEL: Thank you.

COURIER: I will call for you when the Paris train is about to leave and conduct you to your compartment. (*He calls.*) Garçon!

A WAITER *appears.*

WAITER: Monsieur?

COURIER: You wish for coffee or chocolate, sir—milady?

AXEL: Serena?

SERENA: Coffee, please. With milk.

AXEL: Black for me, black and hot and strong.

COURIER: Croissants—an omelette, perhaps?

AXEL: No omelette—just the rolls.

COURIER: Bien, Monsieur. (*To* WAITER.) Croissants, café, vite. Un noir, un blanc, allez.

WAITER: Oui, monsieur!

He scurries away.

COURIER: I trust that milady and monsieur had a pleasant crossing?

AXEL: Lyrical, thank you.

SERENA: I had no idea the Rubicon could be so calm.

COURIER: Pardon, milady.

SERENA: Thank you so much for your courtesy.

COURIER: A pleasure, milady.

AXEL: Her ladyship is travelling incognito. The name is Baxter-Ellis, Mrs. Baxter-Ellis.

COURIER: Entendu, monsieur.

AXEL: Thank you.

COURIER: At your service!

He bows and goes away.

SERENA: What a kind man, and so handsome!

AXEL (*looking at her adoringly*): I could hardly take my eyes off him.

SERENA: Do you always like your coffee black and hot and strong?

AXEL: Yes. It is part of my character—no compromise.

SERENA: How admirable! And how reassuring!

AXEL (*placing his hand over hers on the table*): Do you need reassurance?

SERENA: Oh yes. I'm a prey to agonising fears.

AXEL: What sort of fears, ma'am? Can you name them, or are they the more dangerous kind, unformed and intangible?

SERENA: Quite tangible, based on mistrust.

AXEL: Serena!

SERENA: Not of you, but of Fate; the irrelevant malignancy of the Gods. There might be an earthquake, for instance, the ground might suddenly open and swallow you up before my eyes.

AXEL: Boulogne has not suffered a really serious earthquake for several years.

SERENA: You might have a heart attack.

AXEL: I am having one now. The pain is exquisite!

SERENA: Your heart *is* strong, though, isn't it?

AXEL: It was, but it isn't any more. It is now weak and vulnerable. Before our journey is over you may have to pluck a feather from your hat and burn it under my nose.

The WAITER *appears with the coffee and rolls.*

WAITER: Il y a assez de temps avant le départ, si monsieur desire une omelette.

AXEL: He is a cruel man. He wishes to shame me. His instincts have already told him that I do not understand his damned language.

SERENA: If you want an omelette, nod; if you don't, shake your head and say "Merci".

AXEL: But Merci means thank you.

SERENA: With a shake of the head it means no.

AXEL (*shakes head*): Merci.

WAITER: Bien, monsieur!

He goes.

SERENA: There now!

AXEL: I too have my fears.

SERENA (*pouring out the coffee*): Name them, and they will slink away.

AXEL: The principal one is that you may, in time, become irritated by my roughness, exasperated by my ignorance of your own ingrained tradition and by my lack of grace.

SERENA: I have also dreaded that contingency.

AXEL: You have?

SERENA (*calmly*): I have envisaged desperate possibilities; moments of acute social humiliation when you suddenly attack a soufflé with a knife and fork, or spit

III

into the fireplace without saying Excuse Me. You might also get drunk regularly on Saturday nights and knock me about! When one elopes with an uncivilised ruffian one must be prepared for anything. Here is your coffee, I hope it is black enough.

AXEL (*taking the coffee cup*): I promise never to spit into the fireplace. We will have cuspidors in every room.

SERENA: You may become irritated and exasperated with me first. My "ingrained tradition" may infuriate you one day and turn your heart away from me.

AXEL: I will love you for ever, until the end of time.

SERENA: You said that in Kew Gardens only the other day. Do you remember?

AXEL: You said the same, word for word.

SERENA: You were seen there by a friend of Harriet's! It seems that you were accompanied by a mysterious lady, heavily veiled. I do hope it was the same day!

At this moment MR. SPEVIN, *who has suddenly caught sight of* SERENA *over the top of his newspaper, rises from his table and comes eagerly across to them.*

MR. S.: Lady Heronden!

SERENA (*startled*): Good heavens!

MR. S.: What a delightful coincidence! Mr. Diensen.

AXEL: How do you do, sir.

MR. S.: Fancy our meeting again so unexpectedly, here of all places—is it not extraordinary?

AXEL: Miraculous.

MR. S. (*to* SERENA): I trust that his lordship is well?

SERENA: I am afraid he is a little under the weather this morning.

MR. S.: Oh, I am so sorry! Nothing serious, I hope?

SERENA: No, Mr. Spevin, nothing serious. He will recover in next to no time.

MR. S. (*to* AXEL): And Mrs. Diensen?

AXEL: My wife is in America. She had to visit her lawyers, a family matter.

MR. S.: Ah yes, I see. (*After a slight pause.*) We are on our way home to England for a week or so. My daughter Gwendolyn has been seedy for some time, poor child; the Riviera climate never really agreed with her, so we are taking her to my sister in Abergavenny.

SERENA: The contrast alone should work wonders.

MR. S.: The Welsh air is very bracing; it will soon bring the roses back to her cheeks. It is her stomach, you know.

SERENA: No, I fear I didn't.

MR. S.: The poor mite seems unable to keep anything down.

SERENA: How worrying for you!

MR. S.: Are you on your way to Paris?

AXEL: We are returning to the Villa Zodiaque.

MR. S.: How delightful! Such a view!

SERENA: Our last visit was so brief, but so agreeable, that we felt that we really must go back.

MR. S.: Poor Lady Bonnington will be so pleased. She leads such a lonely life. Does she know you are coming?

AXEL: If I know anything of her inner voices, she'll meet us at the station.

MR. S.: Well, well, well, I must not keep you! My wife and Gwendolyn are already on board. They will be wondering what has happened to me. I hope for the child's sake that the sea is calm.

AXEL: It is, Mr. Spevin. Calm as a mill-pond; the air

too is tranquil and sweet and there is no threat in the sky. In fact the whole world is benign today, gay and smiling.

SERENA (*warningly*): Mr. Diensen!

AXEL: On such a morning as this even Gwendolyn should be able to keep at least something down!

SERENA (*holding out her hand*): Good-bye, Mr. Spevin, and bon voyage!

MR. S.: Thank you so much, your ladyship. My wife will be so sorry to have missed you.

SERENA: Remember me to her.

AXEL: Good luck, Mr. Spevin.

MR. S. (*backing away*): Thank you—thank you—such a pleasure to have seen you again—such a great pleasure. . . .

He grabs up his hat from his table and goes out.

AXEL: Poor Gwendolyn.

SERENA: I remember her at the jumble sale. She wore glasses, her petticoat showed beneath her dress and she won the egg and spoon race.

AXEL: The sun is coming up, the dawn of our first day together.

SERENA: Yes—yes, I know.

AXEL: If this were a dream you would tell me, wouldn't you? You wouldn't let me go on sleeping in foolish bliss until some clanging bell dragged me awake?

A bell rings outside on the platform.

SERENA: There it is. There's your bell.

AXEL: I am still sleeping. Now I know that I shall never wake.

SERENA: Oh dear!

AXEL: What is it?

114

SERENA: Was it wise of us to choose the Villa Zodiaque, I wonder, or was it an error in taste?

AXEL: We have to go there, taste or no taste—it is where we fell in love.

SERENA: This year has been so long I can scarcely remember.

AXEL: I can. Every moment is burned into my brain, every gesture you made, every word you uttered.

SERENA: Did you know—about me, I mean? Did you hear, behind my words, the pounding of my stricken heart?

AXEL: Yes.

SERENA: Oh!

AXEL: Do you resent such unmannerly eaves-dropping?

SERENA: I tried so hard to keep my secret. What waste of time!

AXEL: Every moment of our lives has been waste of time till now.

SERENA: Stuff and nonsense, my darling.

AXEL: You haven't eaten a thing.

SERENA: Neither have you.

AXEL: We shall be hungry in the train.

SERENA: I know. I am looking forward to it.

There is the sound of an engine whistle.

AXEL: That is a warning.

SERENA: Do your beloved American locomotives whistle so hysterically?

AXEL: No, ma'am, they sound a deeper note, more mournful. They have vaster distances to travel, wilder territories to cross and heavier, more virile responsi-bilities: they have no time for shrill, Gallic petulance.

SERENA: The New World. The Brave New World!

115

Will it accept me, do you think? Or shall I be an anachronism?

AXEL: Your earlier adventurers contributed much to its quality, part of your blood is there, so you have a stake in it.

SERENA: You are all the guarantee I need.

AXEL: You will find memories of old England in the most outlandish places.

SERENA: I can scarcely wait. . . .

AXEL: Do not doubt the warmth of your welcome. We are young in heart and eager to enchant our visitors.

SERENA: If only you and I were younger! If only there were more time——

AXEL: There is time enough, my dear love. Time and to spare. Come.

SERENA rises from the table. AXEL takes her hand. There are sounds of whistles blowing, steam escaping, and the clanging of bells.

The COURIER appears in the doorway.

AXEL offers SERENA his arm; she takes it, and with her other hand gathers up her dress. . . . There is a flood of sunshine as they go out on to the platform.

CURTAIN.

116